Language, Intelligence, and Thought

By the same author

Utilitarianism: A contemporary statement (Edward Elgar)
Happiness (Martin Robertson and St. Martin's Press)
Radical Education (Martin Robertson and John Wiley)
Common Sense and the Curriculum (Allen & Unwin)
Moral Philosophy for Education (Allen & Unwin)
Introduction and Commentary on Plato's Apology (JACT)
Plato, Utilitarianism and Education (Routledge & Kegan Paul)
Plato and Education (Routledge & Kegan Paul)
Language and Thought (The Althouse Press)
The Canadian Curriculum (The Althouse Press)
Sparta (Allen & Unwin)
Greek and Roman Education (Macmillan)
Athenian Democracy (Macmillan)
The Philosophy of Schooling (Wheatsheaf and Halsted Press)
Injustice, Inequality, and Ethics (Harvester and Barnes & Noble)
Giving Teaching Back to Teachers (Wheatsheaf, Barnes & Noble and The Althouse Press)
Understanding Skills: Thinking, feeling, and caring (The Althouse Press)

(With R.G. Woods) *Introduction to Philosophy of Education* (Routledge)

(With Geoffrey Milburn) *A Critical Dictionary of Educational Concepts* (Wheatsheaf and Barnes & Noble)

(With Pat White, eds) *Beyond Liberal Education* (Routledge)

For my mother, Awdry Gilchrist Barrow (née Wrightson),
with love.

Contents

Preface

I am particularly indebted to Drs Sharon Bailin, Kieran Egan (both of Simon Fraser University, BC), and John Gingell (Nene College, Northampton), each of whom read the penultimate draft of this book with evident care. Interestingly, with one exception, no comment (friendly or unfriendly) made by any one of them was endorsed by either of the others. Thus, while many points in the argument were criticized by somebody, none of it (with the exception noted) was consistently condemned. In some cases this caused no problem: only one individual might have made the observation, none the less something clearly needed correction or improvement. In other cases, however, I had to decide whether to be sensitive to the concerns of one, or trust in the judgement of two. On the whole I did the latter. It will be evident therefore that on this occasion there is considerable truth in the conventional cry that 'the faults are my responsibility alone'.

Victor Quinn (Bretton Hall, Leeds) kindly read the typescript at the final hour, and I have therefore not been able to do justice to all of his constructive criticism. I should, however, mention his concern that much of my argument, particularly about psychology, applies to North America but not to the UK. He has a point, I think, although it can be overstated. But my reaction is to stress that while it is obviously important that some such views as I criticize should be held by someone, my main concern is with contributing to clear argument on the subject, regardless of who actually holds what views at a particular time in a particular place.

Surjeet Siddoo has worked assiduously at the word processor in preparing this text, as she has on many previous occasions. But this time, even more than usually, if that is possible, her help has been invaluable as we have wrestled with the task of preparing camera ready copy. I can only record my profound gratitude for her patience, skill, and commitment over the years.

PART I

Intelligence

1. The Educated Intelligence

Largely Procedural

Imagine a man who lacks any noteworthy academic credentials, who is more or less ignorant of history (be it of the dawn of civilization, events leading to the Second World War, or his own country), who reads little more than the occasional thriller and newspaper, who is not particularly well informed on current affairs, and who has only a rudimentary understanding of general scientific theory. But suppose also that this man is a very good gardener (he has what some would call green fingers), that he runs a successful landscaping business, that he is religious and has some understanding of church doctrine and affairs, that he is kind and sensitive in his dealings with people, generally adjudged an excellent husband and father, and that he is blessed with the knack of swift and amusing repartee such that many would say he has a quick wit.

Now contrast this man with his brother and two sisters. His elder sister, also somewhat lacking in terms of formal education and quite without interest in the arts, is a highly successful (certainly wealthy) businesswoman. She lacks the light touch and witty response in conversation, but she is very knowledgeable about international politics and current affairs, and can be relied upon to get things done efficiently and well in the day-to-day practical sphere. The younger brother is a successful academic, whose personal life is somewhat erratic and who has no obvious practical skills. He is generally thought to be clever and is not an uninteresting companion, but he lacks the sparkle of his brother and the solid common-sense of his elder sister.

The other sister, like the academic brother, went to university and is well read in literature and history. She started adult life as director of a museum, switched to publishing, and then, in mid-life, started all over again, taking law exams, and became a solicitor. In each stage of her professional life she proved herself extremely capable, but her private life has always been unsatisfactory (even in her own view): she is in fact rather lonely and finds it hard to communicate with other people except in a rather serious, usually professional, manner.

The questions I want to pose are: which, if any, of these individuals should we be inclined to call intelligent? And on what grounds should we make our judgement? Or is the evidence so far provided inadequate to make a judgement, perhaps even altogether the wrong kind of evidence?

Some would say that it is the right kind of evidence, for how else are we to judge people's intelligence if not by reference to what they do and how they live their lives? Amongst this group, however, there might be differences of opinion as to the relevance of different bits of the evidence. To some the reference to quickness of wit would seem to be quintessential, to some the degree of success in life, whether personal or professional, would be considered more important, while to others the question of a more academic kind of knowledge would be crucial. An entirely different group of judges might argue that all the details given are strictly speaking irrelevant: a person's intelligence is not necessarily reflected in how they conduct themselves, still less in their success in life. After all, it may be said, it is quite possible to be intelligent but hugely unsuccessful (due to circumstances beyond one's control), and lacking in confidence, rather sad, and anti-social as a result. Or again, one might be intelligent but lack wisdom, or intelligent but impractical. On this sort of view, one is likely to conclude that estimates of intelligence have to be made by administering some kind of generic test that does not presuppose knowledge of particular subject matter or specific practical abilities. Hence the claim that some people can be shown to have considerable intelligence which they never successfully utilize in terms of their daily lives.

Whatever our particular views on these and similar issues, it is certain that they must be resolved before one could sensibly and meaningfully answer the original question: which, if any, of these individuals could we reasonably call more or less intelligent? You cannot talk about intelligence, make claims as to whether somebody has it, or research into matters relating to it, if you don't have some clear idea of what it is. In just the same way, you cannot reasonably inquire into whether married people are more happy than unmarried people, substantiate the claim that certain people are happy, or talk about the value of happiness, if you cannot give some account of what it means to say that someone is happy. The point can be generalized: you cannot do or say anything about anything (call it x) unless you can provide some definition of x.[1]

So much will be generally admitted. 'I have just discovered that all well-educated people went to private schools' will be widely and correctly dismissed, not as a false, but as an absurd claim, a meaningless one, if the speaker turns out to be incapable of explaining what constitutes being well educated. However, this crucial point needs to be qualified and slightly more fully elaborated, if only because it *is* generally recognized and therefore, in practice, people very seldom make such a crass error. They *do* have 'some idea' of what they mean by 'well educated', 'happy', or 'intelligent'. The question therefore becomes, more specifically, what kind of a definition does one need before one can proceed to make judgements about something? How should one proceed to arrive at a definition, and in what terms should it be given? It is clear enough from daily experience and a casual scrutiny of arguments, claims, and research, that, while virtually everybody acknowledges that you need to have some idea of what it is you are making claims about, people have very different ideas as to what counts as 'some idea'.

It has been argued, quite correctly, that the process of empirical investigation can serve as a means of defining something. The chemist in the laboratory finds out more about a drug through experimentation, and by so doing refines our understanding of the nature of that drug, of what its properties are. The historian, by sustained historical inquiry, modifies and redefines certain historical concepts. The educationalist studying gifted children gradually comes to a more precise understanding of what is involved in being gifted. So much is granted. But three important and major qualifications must be noted.

First, it is in fact very seldom the case that empirical research throws up evidence for some universal characteristic of the object of inquiry, and, even if it does, it does not necessarily follow that this characteristic should be part of the definition. We do not usually come across findings of the type 'all married people are happy; all unmarried people are unhappy'. Far more usual would be some positive correlation that, in ordinary language, amounts to saying something like 'most married people are happier than most unmarried people'. But that, if it were true, would obviously not lead to the conclusion that we should define happiness in terms of being married. In saying that most married people are happier, we are acknowledging that some are not: if it is possible to be married and unhappy, then being married cannot be part of the definition of being happy. More to the point, even if it were the case (*mirabile dictu*) that all married people were always happy and all unmarried people always unhappy, it still would not follow automatically that being married was part of the meaning of being happy. One could decide to make it part of the definition, so that being happy comes to mean something like 'being in a state of benign equilibrium within the state of marriage'. But we would be much more likely to conclude that happiness is to be defined as 'being in a state of benign equilibrium', and that it is an interesting contingent fact that the only way (and an infallible way) of attaining it is through marriage.[2] The important point is that whichever way we go, it is not dictated by the empirical finding. Thus, whether empirical research into intelligence helps us to define the concept more precisely is not a question that the research itself enables us to answer. The most that can be said is that empirical data relating to a concept may suggest redefinition of the concept to us. But whether or not to act upon this suggestion is something that must be decided by what is commonly called philosophical reflection.

Secondly, the help that empirical inquiry may indirectly provide in the task of conceptualizing something is probably proportional to the degree that the concept in question is of something material as opposed to abstract. A chemical, after all, is a physical substance. We may indeed get a more precise understanding of its constituent properties through observation and experiment in the laboratory, and these properties may well become part of the definition of the substance (though whether they do would still be a matter of reflective decision-making). In the same way, if we were to discover that all cows, as normally defined, have some hitherto undetected organ in their bodies and that no other animal had such an organ, we could decide either to make this a part of the definition of a cow or to record it as an invariable fact about cows, defined in the traditional way. But intelligence being abstract, more complex, and more contentious a concept (akin to happiness rather than a cow in these respects), the case is altogether different. If we were to discover (which is emphatically not the case) that all persons whom we were otherwise disposed to call intelligent invariably had an IQ of 150 or over, we surely wouldn't thereby be tempted to say that being intelligent means, amongst other things, having such an IQ. It doesn't mean that: it simply is not the case that what we are trying to say about somebody when we call them intelligent is that they perform to a certain standard on a particular test. In the circumstances depicted, the IQ test would provide us with an infallible indicator of intelligence, but good performance on the test wouldn't be intelligence, just as a thermometer gives us an infallible reading of the temperature but is not to be confused with the temperature itself.

Thirdly, even though, in the limited ways referred to, empirical research may help us indirectly to refine our conceptions, it remains the case that one cannot begin the research without some idea of what one is researching into: some definition arrived at by reflective philosophical analysis rather than by any kind of empirical inquiry is a necessary precondition of empirical inquiry.

We thus come again to the questions of what kind of an idea will suffice and how, in more precise terms, does one arrive at an idea that is adequate or sufficient for the purposes of further inquiry, including empirical research.

We cannot give a general answer in quantitative terms to the question of how much of an idea is sufficient to count as 'some idea'. It depends upon factors such as what kind of an idea we are dealing with and what we intend to do with it. But what we can do is indicate the criteria that an appropriate conceptualization ought to meet (in practical terms come as near to as possible), and, equally important, draw attention to some ways of explaining ideas that are quite inappropriate and that need to be avoided, despite their popularity. Prominent amongst the techniques to be avoided are the use of metaphor, analogy, example, behavioural definition, and simple verbal synonyms. Rather, we need to expound a conception by reference to the four criteria of clarity, coherence, completeness, and compatibility with our other ideas and beliefs. (For the obvious reason, I refer to these criteria as the Four Cs of analysis.)[3]

Let us imagine that our interest is in happiness and that we are trying to articulate some account of what we take 'happiness' to mean, or happiness to be, prior to investigating various hypotheses as to what sorts of thing make what sorts of people happy. We can now illustrate in greater detail both the moves to be avoided and those with which we should be concerned.

It will not be adequate to say in response to the question, 'What do I mean by happiness?', 'Well, I mean by happiness the sort of feeling that I have when I fall in love' or 'The sort of disposition that my friends Fred and Ginger, whom everybody agrees are happy, have'. This kind of approach will not do because, quite apart from obvious difficulties such as that nobody but you knows how you feel, and that we don't know whether Fred and Ginger are truly happy, whatever everybody agrees, it is not answering the question at all. To give examples both begs the question of whether they are in fact truly examples and at the same time fails to provide us with any means of determining that, since it says nothing about why they should count as examples. Why is the feeling that I have when I fall in love to be classified as a feeling of happiness? That is the question. Examples can be useful as part of a much larger strategy, but they are only useful in so far as one mines them to extract criteria for determining whether something is to count as an instance of happiness (or whatever the concept may be).

Metaphors and analogies, if they are all we provide and if we do nothing to analyse them, are likewise a way of avoiding the challenge. If I want to know what you mean by happiness, then learning that it is like being high on a drug may not only be unilluminating to me (if, for example, I have never taken drugs), but also fails to tell me precisely what I want to know: granted that it is in some way like being high on a drug, how does it differ? Everybody knows that happiness refers to some kind of euphoric sense, some sense of well-being. What we need to know is something about its distinctive nature, something about what distinguishes it from other similar but different states of mind.

Behavioural definitions are fine in their place. And their place is to be found when we are concerned with matters that are exclusively matters of behaviour. A behavioural definition of politeness, for example, would be entirely in order, since being polite is entirely a matter of behaving in certain ways. It has nothing to do with how you feel or your motives for so behaving. But, in our example, happiness is clearly not exclusively a matter of behaviour. Conceivably one might cry all day, shout at people, rail at the world, and still be happy. There is no set of specific behaviours that is sufficient to establish that a person is happy by definition, and no particular behaviour (I think) that is necessary to what we mean by happiness.[4] So, in this case, a behavioural definition would be positively misleading.

Simple verbal synonyms merely exchange one perplexing word or set of words for another perplexing word or set of words. If I don't know what a 'dog' is, telling me that it is a *'chien'* won't help at all. Of course, for many simple ideas, when our problem is simply lack of familiarity with certain vocabulary, verbal synonyms and other kinds of dictionary definition are entirely satisfactory. I may not be familiar with the word 'pulchritude', but I will be entirely satisfied with the explanation that it's another word for 'physical beauty'. And while the words 'induction coil' are both individually familiar to me, I may need to be told that the phrase refers to 'a transformer for producing high voltage from low voltage'. But my problem with happiness and intelligence is not of this kind. I know what the words mean at the level of vocabulary: 'intelligence' is the same as the Greek *'nous'* and the French *'intelligence'*; it refers to mental ability, and it might be glossed as the capacity for understanding. That much I know. My problem, and our problem, if we want to research it, is that whatever word or words I use, the idea is still too obscure to allow us to do such things as regularly recognize it.[5]

Operational definitions are, or may be, subversive creatures. The argument often goes: 'I am a researcher wanting to research into happiness. But since I want to conduct a certain kind of research I must have a definition in terms that lend themselves to my kind of research. I will call it operational to indicate it is a definition designed to suit my operating needs and that I do not lay claim to having captured the essence of happiness. But it will at least be clear what I am researching into'. Well, of course it will. But what a pity you called it 'happiness', if in fact it has nothing to do with happiness. And how confused the world will be when your research is summarized as establishing that happy people are generally male, whereas in fact you merely established that males smile a lot.

What is required is philosophical analysis, an approach which, despite its manifest importance as a necessary foundation for all other forms of inquiry, has something of a bad name in certain quarters today. I attribute this to three main factors. First, it is a very general term covering a variety of quite distinct species. (Or, to put it another way, it means different things to different people.) Secondly, some types of analysis deserve a bad name, being, for one reason or another, very implausible ways of approaching the question of what something such as 'intelligence' means. Thirdly, as a consequence of the first two points, much actual analysis is of very little practical help.

Two types of analysis that deserve particular mention as species to be avoided are linguistic analysis and essentialist analysis. In fact I doubt whether many, if any, philosophers are guilty of being wedded to either of these heresies in the extreme form that I am concerned with. But, since there is widespread criticism of philosophical analysis on the mistaken grounds that it necessarily involves one or both of these approaches, they need to be mentioned.

The view that merely by analysing the way a word is used we arrive at a proper understanding of a concept is quite untenable. Clearly, the way people use the word may be muddled, confused, and even contradictory. Besides, at best this tells us what a group of language users mean; it tells us what they think about intelligence or whatever. But what they think may be nonsensical. How words are used is obviously something that should be given close consideration, and it will generally reveal data that should be grist to the philosophical mill. But it cannot be more than one technique among others. Other criteria have to be used to decide where and in what respects usage should be our guide.

Of more significance to the overall argument of this book is a repudiation of the so-called essentialist view. This is the view that there is a definitive correct answer to a question of the form 'what is x?', or that there is a true conception of, for example, intelligence, in some sense out there waiting to be captured, brought to earth, and dissected by the philosopher. More will be said about this later, but here it should be clearly stated that I am assuming that, while silly, unacceptable, unconvincing, etc., conceptions of abstract ideas such as happiness and intelligence may be offered, the presumption that there is a true or correct conception is to be resisted. It is not so much that the question of truth or falsity does not arise, as that it is irrelevant to this inquiry. Our concern is to come to grips with concepts that we do have, rather than to argue about whether (and therefore in what sense) they are true, real, have existence, and so on.

Our task, starting from the hazy and vague idea of intelligence that we share, since we are brought up in a common culture conveyed by a common language, is to get as full a grasp as we can of that concept, knocking some shape into it along the way. In attempting to explicate the idea, we need to be guided not by any concern for its truth or reality in the abstract, but by a concern that the concept be clear, coherent, and complete in the sense of articulated as fully as possible; and that, when it has been unpacked in this way, it should be compatible with our other concepts and the other beliefs that we hold.

More will be said about these criteria in the pages that follow *(see pp. 37 - 41)*. I shall seek to unfold a conception of intelligence that meets the criteria, indicating along the way why much of the psychological inquiry into intelligence is not so much mistaken as irrelevant to our concerns, certainly as educators, perhaps more widely. I shall conclude by pointing out the implications for education and for our judgement as to the relative intelligence of the four siblings introduced at the beginning of this chapter.

I have said that the question of the truth or falsity of my (or any other) conception of intelligence is irrelevant. But I should make it clear that this means neither that there are no criteria, so that anything goes, nor that in some more general sense I am unconcerned about questions of truth.

Anything does not go. Or, if that is bad English, let me rephrase it: it is not the case that anything goes in this sphere, if that means that you can define intelligence in any way that you like. Of course you can't. First, there is the word. The word 'intelligence' does not mean 'stupid', or 'red-haired', or 'suave'. If we are talking about 'intelligence' we are talking about something to do with 'understanding' or 'mental ability'. If you think otherwise you are mistaken. Your mistake is purely verbal (rather than conceptual), but it is a mistake none the less. You do not understand the English language. Secondly, what you can reasonably say in your attempt to analyse this so far general and vague idea of intelligence is severely limited both by the four criteria referred to and by our understanding of what the facts of the matter are. To say that the truth or falsity of an analysis is irrelevant is to say that if two people, both playing by the rules, come up with distinguishable conceptions, neither of which can be faulted in respect of lack of clarity, coherence, completeness, or compatibility, nor in respect of the way things are, then both are plausible and we have no way of adjudicating between them. Such an occurrence is unlikely, given the fact of widely shared networks of belief that will have a strong bearing on the issue of compatibility, but it is conceivable. But in any event, as I hope is clear even at this introductory stage, the claim that one cannot dismiss a conception as false in no way implies that one cannot legitimately criticize a conception as inadequate.

The related question of what style of definition is to be preferred, it is perhaps worth reminding ourselves, is a question to be answered by reference both to the nature of the concept and to our purposes or interests. A behavioural definition, for example, can only be justified by the fact that a concept is behavioural by nature, or for a limited purpose such as observational research (but note the warning sounded above). The question of whether, for example, we should prefer a definition of intelligence in terms of mental process or consequent achievements is to be decided partly by our understanding of the concept in itself, but partly by reference to what it is that we value and whether we wish the concept to prove useful in various respects. To anticipate what will be argued in greater detail below: a view of intelligence as a mental process is not to be dismissed as false, but it may be pointed out that a conception in this form makes intelligence a somewhat useless and perhaps valueless concept, since we cannot say much about the process or observe it in action, and there is no obvious reason to value the process in itself.

As to truth more generally, of course I am very much concerned with it. It would be foolish to deny the very idea of truth and related concepts such as objectivity. Indeed, even a strong claim to the effect that all is relative is presumably put forward on the grounds that it is true in some objective sense. By all means let us draw attention to historical and cultural difference, and let us acknowledge that all claims to knowledge are provisional. But that is a far cry from suggesting that we should not aim for truth and in so doing continue to value logic, evidence, and rationality.

One further comment seems in order here: we spend so much time arguing about what are sometimes called meta-theoretical issues that we are in danger of forgetting to get on with the job. While we discuss philosophy of science, we fail to do science; while we debate deconstructionism, we cease to read literature; while we discuss philosophical technique, we avoid using it; while we argue about the nature of educational theory and research, we don't do any. More generally, so long as we allow ourselves to be distracted by rather sterile and unconvincing arguments about truth, we are losing opportunities to acquire such true understanding as we can.

Thesis and Method

According to the argument of this book, language, thought, and intelligence are very closely related concepts. Not only does what is meant by intelligence overlap considerably with what is meant by the capacity to think and with what is meant by command of language (which are themselves closely interrelated), but in practice people's ability to proceed intelligently through life is largely dictated by their ability to think well, which, in turn, is by and large co-extensive with their mastery of verbal language. If this is true, and if we want to produce intelligent adults, it follows that schools need, in broad terms, to concentrate on developing the individual's command of language. And if that is true, it follows that we need to give consideration to what is meant by 'command of language' in this context. In the light of that consideration we can proceed to make more reasonable and precise judgements about the educational value of various competing suggestions about pedagogy and the school curriculum.

The thesis that I shall advance and seek to substantiate may be summarized as follows: in one sense of the word, intelligence is something that can be developed and enhanced, and intelligence in this sense is something that ought to be a prime concern of educators. Developing intelligence, in this sense, is essentially a matter of developing the individual's capacity to think well, and that in turn is essentially a matter of developing the individual's linguistic ability. The language in question is verbal, rather than, say, pictorial or musical, if indeed it is reasonable to talk of music or painting as languages. The appropriate way to develop this linguistic ability is to provide a version of what has for a long time been referred to as a liberal education: specifically, but at this stage still in broad terms, an education that immerses the individual in a range of powerful traditions of inquiry and exegesis about the world and the human condition.

As noted above, if this thesis were to be fully understood and accepted, it would put us in a position, as would any coherent account of the aims of education, to judge the appropriateness of particular curricular and pedagogical proposals. One of the oddities of much contemporary educational research is that it professes to have established that particular practices are desirable or undesirable, are effective or not effective, work or do not work, without paying much direct attention to the question of what counts as educational success. But whether a certain procedure is effective depends partly on the empirical question of what it leads to and partly on the non-empirical evaluative question of what is important. To have a clear idea of the aims of education, of what it is to be well educated, is therefore necessary to any claim about good and bad means or practices. The thesis in question provides an account of what would count as a well-educated person, and would therefore put us in a position to evaluate practices. However, it is not my intention to pursue those questions in any detail in this book. I shall be content if I can provide a sufficiently clear account of the thesis and the argument to support it, such as to convince readers of its plausibility.

The following chapters will take us step by step through the argument, but here it seems advisable to make a few preliminary comments on the summary of the thesis given above and, in particular, to talk about the methodology or nature of the argument that I shall employ.

I claim that there is a sense of the word 'intelligence' that makes it both something that can be developed and something educationally desirable. The significance of this claim is that many people, no doubt partly as a result of the dominance of psychological inquiry in education, think of intelligence as a more or less fixed and given capacity - something that cannot be much improved or reduced. The individual is presumed to be born with a certain degree of intelligence and, within narrow limits, to retain it to his or her dying day. The most familiar instance of such thinking is provided by those who equate intelligence with IQ, and who believe that IQ tests more or less adequately judge this innate quality. For the moment we do not need to concern ourselves with possible criticisms of IQ testing. It is sufficient to say that, even were there to be some relatively constant mental capacity which might be identified with IQ, we would be under no obligation to define intelligence in terms of IQ.

In point of fact different people use the word 'intelligence' in a variety of different ways, and at least some of the traditional judgements on the intelligence of people clearly have nothing to do with IQ, if only because they are made in reference to people about whose IQ we do not know, or by people who know nothing about IQ testing. The judgement that Plato, for example, was a highly intelligent man has nothing to do with his IQ, about which we know absolutely nothing. The judgement of some that Winston Churchill was highly intelligent would not be upset by the news that he had a low IQ. What this boils down to, for us, is the need to recognize at the outset that there are different senses or uses of the word 'intelligence', that each distinct sense could be said to represent a different conception, and that what matters is to adopt a conception that we are able to argue has educational value. As we shall see, one problem with identifying intelligence with IQ, or with relating our conception closely to some such innate and unalterable quality, is that it is not clear why we should particularly value a high intelligence in this sense, nor what relevance it has to educational practice, since, by definition, it cannot be significantly altered. Why, for example, should I admire members of Mensa, just because they have high IQs? Why, as a teacher, should I concern myself about the IQ of at any rate the majority of my students, given that they will fall roughly in a broad middle band of distribution and there is little or nothing I can do to improve them?[6]

The thesis, then, clearly demands that I give some account of what kind of intelligence, or what sense of the word 'intelligence', I am concerned with, and produce some argument for the educational value of such intelligence. I shall do this by setting out a definition of the word in terms of thinking of high quality, and, of course, in doing this I shall need to convince readers that the characteristics of high-quality thinking that I identify are indeed such.

The next point to draw attention to is my use of the word 'essentially', by which I mean something like 'in crucial respects' and 'to all practical intents and purposes'. In other words, I will be arguing that if we take steps to improve an individual's command of language in a particular identifiable sense (and that sense will be identified), then we will thereby improve the individual's capacity to think well, and that capacity will be more or less identifiable with intelligence in the desired sense. The overall argument will be partly a matter of logic, arising out of conceptual links, and partly a matter of empirical facts. But it should be noted here that I do not claim that 'intelligence', 'linguistic command',

and 'thinking capacity' are simply synonymous terms; nor do I claim that individuals with a good command of language will necessarily think well, still less proceed intelligently; nor do I claim that people cannot proceed intelligently, if they cannot express themselves well linguistically. The matter is far too complex to allow of any such categorical statements. What I do maintain and hope to establish is that there is nothing that we should more obviously do than concentrate on developing language competence, if we want to enhance people's ability to live their lives intelligently.

The explicit reference to verbal language is made at this early stage to give warning that while I am naturally aware that claims are sometimes made to the effect that some people do not think verbally, or that intelligence can be manifested, say, in visual or auditory terms, I do not believe that such vague claims can be substantiated in any meaningful way. At worst the notion of thinking visually does not make sense; at best such a capacity, if it does exist, would constitute a private language of no use for intelligent intercourse and communication with fellow beings. Or so I shall argue.

A methodological point now needs to be made. It follows on my observation that part of the overall argument is not empirical and my reference to the fact that much educational research is conducted without reference to any notion of educational success. The dominance of empirical research in education, arising partly no doubt out of the productivity and real value of much work in the field, may tend to leave the unwary with the idea that on the one hand we have objective facts that are empirical in nature, and on the other we have various forms of subjective, and hence arbitrary, opinion.

But this is wrong in all sorts of important way. First, not all facts or truths are empirical: that the angles of a triangle add up to 180 degrees, that I am writing these words, that I am happy at the moment, are all facts or truths as certain as we can hope to get, but none of them can be directly proven by empirical means. (There are empirical considerations that may be relevant to determining the truth of such claims, but in the end they cannot be empirically demonstrated.)[7] Secondly, not all empirical claims, even when supported by extensive and respected research, are true. Whether claims are true depends on whether they correspond to the facts, whether what is claimed is in fact the case.[8] How one determines whether something is true has nothing to do with its truth or objectivity. One adopts (or should adopt) a methodology (whether a species of empirical or non-empirical), not by reference to a theory about the best way to determine truth in general, but by reference to the nature of a particular claim. If the claim is about something directly observable, one observes; if it is presumed to be a deduction, then one deduces; if it is allegedly a logical necessity, one examines the logic.

A possible line of criticism of current educational research is therefore that the dominance of empirical work, with the accompanying error of assuming that the empirical is necessarily more certain, has led to our placing too much trust in empirical claims, to the marginalizing of various very important but non-empirical questions, and in some cases the distortion of questions. Thus, we believe that a given style of teaching is desirable because it is backed by a wealth of empirical study, forgetting that no amount of empirical study alone could show anything to be desirable, since desirability is not itself an empirically demonstrable quality. Thus, we shy away from and ignore vital questions such as, in particular, questions of value, since, when we are not improperly smuggling value judgements in, as in the previous example, we imagine them to be a mere matter of whim or opinion. And thus we tend to turn to empirical studies of intelligence, without recognizing that the concept of intelligence has been largely distorted in that domain, in order to render it something that can be empirically studied. Just as much research into what makes for a happy marriage is in point of fact no such thing - it is research into observable behaviour, such as what makes people smile, avoid complaining, or say they are happy, that is certainly not identifiable with the emotional state of happiness, even if on some occasions it may serve as a reliable indicator of that state - so a great deal of research into intelligence, though it may be technically sound and have a value of its own, has little or nothing to do with any plausible account of intelligence.

Philosophy, too, which ought to provide the necessary balance to unthinking empiricism, is to be criticized, partly for its failure to bring itself to bear on empirical research, and partly because, as we have seen, it is sometimes defined in ways that diminish its credibility.

The fact is that most educational questions are a hybrid of empirical and non-empirical elements. Questions to do with intelligence are no exception. Their proper examination requires an exposure of the extent to which, heretofore, empirical research has tended to be conducted without an adequate philosophical base, the articulation of an adequate conception of intelligence, the detailed exploration of the various logical implications of such a conception, and the subsequent adoption of whatever empirical means are available to us that suit the nature of the concept to research further contingent questions about intelligence.

An Educational Goal

In order to set the argument of this book in a clear and manageable context, I want first to set forth an educational goal that will, I hope, gain fairly widespread assent. If we can agree on something that is central to what we want to achieve in the process of educating students, and relate what follows to the achievement of that aim, then the significance and practical importance of the argument will be evident, even when the argument itself seems rather abstract and theoretical.

The goal I have in mind is that of producing or developing individuals who can think autonomously and critically about important matters, and who understand both the nature and the limits of human understanding in its current state. As I shall argue below, this aim of education might be put more succinctly as the aim of producing intelligent adults. But, for the moment, I shall stick with the more detailed and lengthy description (since many people would not define 'intelligence' in those terms), and begin by explaining and qualifying the account of the goal.

My assumption is that few would actually oppose the idea of wanting students to become autonomous, understanding, critical thinkers. Many would, of course, immediately want to add much more to the goal. What about the need to produce good citizens, to socialize individuals, to develop the body as well as the mind, to cultivate the emotions and aesthetic sensibility? And what about the process of education? Should we not make reference to such things as learning how to learn, the process of inquiry, the happiness of the student? Some might even say that my goal is far too idealistic and academic: what about preparing individuals for the world of work?

But these other concerns need not detain us here, provided that we agree that the goal I have outlined represents a part of what we want to achieve. My own view is that most, if not all, of the other goals mentioned are also important, though many of them are much more closely bound up with the intellectual goal I am stressing than is sometimes realized. For example, cultivating the emotions and aesthetic sensibility is an objective I wholeheartedly endorse, but I would argue that it is inseparable from cultivating understanding: to appreciate a work of art, though it involves other things, necessarily involves understanding art. To be able to love, to recognize and control jealousy, or to master hate in an appropriate manner, likewise is partly dependent on understanding. Indeed, even to recognize an emotion such as jealousy for what it is requires understanding, since jealousy is not simply a sensation but is rather a certain kind of feeling brought on by understanding one's situation to be of a certain sort. But, in any case, whether they are all closely bound up with the capacity to think critically and autonomously or not, I am not here rejecting these or any other possible aims of education. I am only asserting that one plausible and important goal is the one I have outlined.

I refer to 'producing or developing' thinking individuals because I do not wish to get involved in what I regard as rather sterile arguments about whether education should be seen as analogous to filling empty buckets or watering germinating seeds. The answer, fairly obviously, is that it is not very profitable to approach it in terms of metaphors at all. Let us take it for what it is, something unique, and seek to understand it directly rather than by means of imperfect analogies. The fact is that teachers do things to, with, and in front of students, and they encourage students to copy them, do things on their own, experiment, learn things by heart, and so on. And teachers do all these things because, notwithstanding the fact that other things such as the wider environment, parental influence, and genetic make-up of the individual play a part, they have every reason to suppose that what they - the teachers - do also makes a profound difference. Whether it would be more appropriate to see the child as essentially unfolding his or her nature in a congenial atmosphere or as being directed and influenced to a certain end state, I do not know. Nor, I think, does anyone else, although many have strong opinions on the subject. My phrasing allows me to ignore this rather tedious issue: the emphasis falls on the point that what we hope is that by the end of schooling, and no doubt partly as a result of the nature of that schooling, individuals will be capable of sound thinking. It really doesn't matter for our purposes whether we tend to the view that teachers are merely facilitators or see them as playing a more active role.

By 'critical' thinking, I do not mean negative, destructive thinking. In common with all of the many educationalists who are concerned with this notion, despite their many other differences, I mean to refer to the capacity to assess the validity, appropriateness, and relevance of information and argument rather than merely to accept them passively. The critical thinker is one who has a disposition to examine and question the ideas he encounters and to do so in a rational rather than, say, an emotional manner. 'Critical' is thus, in this context, closely related to 'autonomous', which carries the further implication that the individual's critical assessment of ideas shall be authentically his or her own, and not simply a matter of applying critical strategies which have been taken on trust from others or from some ideological system of thought, and are not themselves subjected to scrutiny. In colloquial terms, one might say simply that what is meant by reference to autonomous and critical thought is that the individual shall think for himself, questioning not only the coherence of the matter at hand but also the coherence of the very manner of inquiry employed - in short, taking nothing on trust.

This is both idealized and purely formal. None of us works out everything individually, taking nothing on trust, even over a period of time, and clearly one cannot examine and establish to one's own satisfaction all the presumptions that one works with at the same time as working with them: if I am presented with some new data about smoking and lung cancer, I can attempt to assess its worth for myself, but I cannot realistically at the same time assess for myself the worth of the scientific mode of reasoning that I employ in assessing the new data. But the idealistic nature of the goal in this (and other respects) need not trouble us. Nobody perhaps will ever be completely autonomous and critical, but that does not make it inappropriate for us to conceive of our goal as becoming so. The fact that the account is formal - which is to say it tells us the type of thinking we are concerned with, but does not specify what thinking is in fact critical and autonomous - will ultimately need more consideration, but need not trouble us at this point.

Similarly, and perhaps more obviously, the formal claim that we want people who can think critically about 'important matters' raises the question of what specifically are important matters. This could become a vital issue, since educators might disagree with each other about whether the goal had been met in particular cases, because they disagree about whether the kinds of thing that students are agreed to think critically about are important. But, as before, this admittedly significant point need not prevent us from agreeing now that we would not be satisfied unless our students thought about matters that we considered to be important. Thus, and purely by way of example, I would not consider my job well done if all that my students could reason about were such things as hockey and soap operas, while they remained incapable of participating in debates about fundamental political, ethical, religious, and scientific matters.

The above may be elaborated slightly, if we turn now to the second half of the goal I have set down. I have deliberately used the word 'understanding' rather than 'knowledge' since the latter implies certainty in a way that the former does not. If I truly 'know' that King Henry VIII of England dissolved the monasteries, as opposed to merely believe it, imagine it, guess it, intuit it, or recite the claim, that is to say both that it is the case that Henry dissolved the monasteries and that I understand the reasoning, the evidence, and so forth that shows it to be the case. (One cannot, strictly speaking, be said to know something that is not true or something for the truth of which one has no evidence.) Thus knowledge can only be of what is and of what is fully understood. But there are a great many things, including some very important ones, that can be understood even though they are false or when it is uncertain whether they are true. If astrology is bunkum, for example, then I cannot be said to know any astrological truths, but it is still a subject that one can come to understand. One can understand a religion, without committing oneself to its truth or falsity. One can understand a scientific claim, once thought to be true and hence regarded as knowledge, that turns out to be false. In addition, understanding can be of various degrees, whereas you either know something or you don't. For these reasons my choice of the word 'understanding' is significant. The goal does not suppose that we are aiming to produce individuals who have grasped political, ethical, and aesthetic truth. It implies that there will be individuals who have some understanding of the nature of political, ethical, and aesthetic argument and reasoning. The reference to understanding 'the limits' of our understanding should also be noted: the kind of understanding I am referring to involves, in respect of, for example, the natural sciences, not only understanding how the sciences proceed, but also understanding ways in which the procedures might be fallible and conditions under which they would be quite inappropriate.

Notes and references

1. Note the general phrasing of 'some definition'. It is true that we can treat, e.g., a cold, despite our ignorance of the precise nature, cause, etc., of a cold. However, we obviously could not do so, if we had no idea what we meant by 'a cold'.
2. 'The only and an infallible means' of attaining some object is not to be confused with a logically necessary condition of that object. A certain medicine may be necessary to maintain or restore my health, but it is no part of the definition of my health.
3. The account that I give of philosophical analysis in this book builds on arguments that I have advanced in Barrow, R., (1990), *Understanding Skills*, London, Ontario: Althouse Press; Barrow, R. and Milburn, G., (1990), *A Critical Dictionary of Educational Concepts*, 2nd ed, London: Harvester Wheatsheaf; and elsewhere. An understanding of this position is essential to the argument of this book.
4. See further, Barrow, R., (1980), *Happiness*, Oxford: Martin Robertson.
5. It is not disputed that we have enough of an idea of intelligence to recognize that, e.g., Einstein had intelligence. But even here we often make the attribution without being very clear as to precisely why we do.
6. A possible counter argument would suggest that knowledge of differing IQs might enable the teacher to provide different material to different students or to ensure that an individual's performance was up to par. For reasons that will become apparent in the next three chapters, this line of argument does not impress me.
7. One cannot, for example, measure triangles in order to establish that their angles always add up to 180 degrees, because it is the fact that they do that partly determines whether a particular shape is a true triangle. You would need to be present observing me, to establish empirically that I am now writing these words, and that you cannot be.
8. This is not an endorsement of the so-called correspondence theory of truth.

2. Psychology and Intelligence

Psychological Definitions

As we have seen, defining a word and analysing a concept, though closely related, are none the less distinct activities. Essentially, the difference lies in the fact that defining a word is a matter of providing a synonym or synonymous phrasing, while analysing a concept involves probing, expanding, examining, and unpacking the implications of the idea conveyed by the word or synonymous phrasing. Thus, the dictionary defines 'teacher' as 'a person who teaches; an instructor', which serves its purpose for those who were unfamiliar with the word, but does little else. Analysis of the concept of teacher would involve raising, pursuing, and answering such questions as whether any kind of instruction counts as teaching; whether one might be teaching when not instructing; what in fact 'instructing' means (where does it begin, where does it end?); whether it matters how one instructs. In other words, analysis involves trying to establish a more precise and detailed account of the extent and limits of an idea: what conditions in particular have to be met for an activity to count as teaching, and what conditions would be sufficient for us to classify an activity as teaching (the search for necessary and sufficient conditions).

Analysis can lead one to modify, challenge, or even reject the dictionary definition. One might argue, for instance, that in this case the conclusion to be drawn is that the definition of teaching in terms of instruction is unacceptable. Instruction is neither a necessary part of nor a sufficient characterization of the activity. (Alternatively, one might say that 'instruction' is as vague a word as 'teaching', and the definition of one in terms of the other does nothing to increase our understanding of what either actually involves.) Sometimes, particularly in the case of complex ideas, dictionaries offer more by way of definition than in this example, and occasionally a dictionary entry may approach analysis. Conversely, some analysis requires little more than the provision of a dictionary-type definition. (For example, the concept of a triangle is adequately analysed in the dictionary entry 'a three-sided polygon with angles that add up to 180 degrees'.) But it remains important to recognize the possibility of two distinct activities: providing a synonym and exploring an idea.

Strictly speaking, conceptual analysis is a philosophical task, and, typically, philosophers engage in this activity in a marked and obvious way. But while psychology, science, sociology, history, and so on are to be distinguished from philosophy, and while, again strictly speaking, doing psychology or science is not doing philosophy, in practice other disciplines often engage in some philosophizing and in particular in conceptual analysis. They need to explore their own concepts, and often they do it very well. The problem arises when they do it inadequately, or when what they are doing is misunderstood to be something other than it is.

A case in point arises with intelligence. Few psychologists or sociologists could claim to have contributed much to analysis of the concept. That is to say, they have not explored the concept in the appropriate philosophical manner. What they have done is either made claims about intelligence without explicitly revealing what they take it to mean, or explicitly defined the term in (usually behavioural) ways that are both incomplete and questionable. (Research into giftedness betrays the same pattern: a variety of attempts have been made to define the term, some of which are incoherent, some of which are confused, some of which are unenlightening, and so forth, but none of which really gets to grips with the question of what we suppose it means to call someone gifted. When the definitions are clear, it is not only debatable whether the definition corresponds with what other people mean by the term, it is also quite often arguable that giftedness as it is defined is of no particular interest to us.)[1]

If we examine a selection of psychology textbooks, we get a variety of kinds of answer to the question 'what is intelligence?'. Thus, Gage and Berliner write: 'In a sense everyone knows what intelligence is. It is brightness, "sharpness", ability to solve problems, speed in figuring things out, capacity to learn from experience'.[2] This is a clear example of definition rather than analysis: it offers a variety of synonyms, some of them, such as 'sharpness', being essentially metaphors, and it does not explore or probe the idea of intelligence at all. As they themselves acknowledge, at this level everyone knows what intelligence is. But we need to advance beyond this level to get a clearer and fuller picture of in what exactly this intelligence, this brightness, this problem solving ability, consists. The definition proffered in this case is of very little use.

Furthermore, not only does such an account fail to increase our understanding, in some cases the paraphrases raise more questions than they answer: is there in fact such a thing as a general ability to solve any kind of problem, as seems to be implied, as opposed to the ability to solve certain particular kinds of problem? And what is the nature of this ability in either case?

Is it an innate capacity or something that is acquired? Is speed an essential part of what we mean by intelligence, or might we consider that a person whose response to problems or situations is slow and considered, but shrewd and insightful, was none the less intelligent? Is one intelligent if one has the capacity to learn from experience but does not in fact do so? Or is the implication that the capacity is judged in the light of success? If not, how is it to be judged? If so, how does one reasonably determine that the individual's success is the product of this mysterious capacity rather than such things as learning, other environmental factors, or simply good fortune? To say that intelligence is brightness is to say nothing, to say that it is sharpness is to add nothing to saying that it is brightness. But while those two words are virtually synonymous with each other and with intelligence, ability to solve problems and speed in figuring things out are clearly distinct. Is the claim then that these are alternative ways of characterizing intelligence, or that all are necessary conditions? If the latter, is it in fact the case that an intelligent person must meet all of these and only these criteria?

Lefrancois suggests that non-experts will tend to say that 'intelligent people are the ones who do well at school'.[3] Here it is not clear whether the suggestion is that this would be the non-expert definition, or whether it would be a non-expert claim about a contingent fact, to the effect that intelligent people (defined in some other way) do tend to do well in school. Granted that Lefrancois is not recording his own view but specifically that of non-experts (and assuming he means to imply that it is therefore not worthy of particular respect or attention, which is unclear), the fact remains that this is an instance of a response to the question of what intelligence is that is confusingly ambiguous and, on either interpretation, unimpressive. As a definition it seems most implausible. We simply don't equate school success with intelligence, and don't mean by calling someone intelligent that they were or are successful in school. If we did, we would not be able to make judgements about people's intelligence without knowing their school record, but we do that all the time. Nor would we be able to deny that all individuals with first-class degrees were extremely intelligent, which, one would have thought, we quite certainly and quite often want to deny. On the other hand, as a contingent claim it seems equally questionable. Surely many people do relatively well in school for a whole variety of reasons that have nothing to do with their intelligence, and conversely many people whom we judge to be highly intelligent do not do particularly well in school. At the very least, to make any sort of connection between school success and intelligence one would need to know something about the schooling in question. To be successful in one kind of school with one set of values and goals would betoken something quite different from success in a radically different kind of school.

Harré and Lamb define intelligence as 'the all-round mental ability (or thinking skills) either of human or of lower animal species'.[4] Here again important questions are begged and the verbal synonym style of definition gets us little further in understanding the concept. Is there any good reason to assume that there is such a thing as an 'all-round mental ability'? Is it even a plausible hypothesis, given that very few if any individuals actually show intelligence in all spheres of life? If there is none the less such a thing, what kind of thing is it? And whether there is or is not, in some sense, an all-round mental ability that an individual might have, is it that to which we typically refer when we judge somebody to be intelligent? *Prima facie*, is it not rather the case that we judge people to be intelligent by reference to their understanding of various matters? Similarly, to gloss this putative ability as 'thinking skills' is to beg the question of whether the ability to reason and act intelligently is appropriately characterized in terms of 'skills'. Certainly, the so-called skills of the intelligent historian or intelligent diplomat would seem to be of a very different order from the skills of the first-class cricketer or the *cordon bleu* chef. That is to say, on the face of it, if mental or intellectual abilities are skills, they are skills of a distinctive kind, which raises the question: of what kind are they? Perhaps seemingly less immediately relevant, but in fact of considerable significance, is the question of whether 'lower' animals do have intelligence. They certainly have brains and they certainly act in ways that might be taken to suggest rational thought, calculation, purpose, and so forth. But it is at least debatable whether even monkeys and dogs do actually think in the manner that we assume to betoken intelligence. It might be argued that even apparently sophisticated animals function exclusively in terms of automatic stimulus and response. Admittedly, some psychologists would concede that, but argue that humans also function exclusively in this way, and that the human is merely a particularly sophisticated kind of animal. For our purposes, at this stage, the important thing to note is that this is a highly contentious claim, and that, ultimately, deciding where to draw the line between intelligent behaviour and merely re-active behaviour, while partly a matter of empirical evidence, is also crucially a matter of determining what counts as intelligence. That the monkey uses a stick to draw a piece of fruit through the bars of a cage, for instance, is not in dispute. Whether that necessarily indicates intelligence is far from certain and depends partly on how we characterize intelligence.

Historically there have certainly been modifications and changes to the prevailing psychological accounts of intelligence, and psychologists themselves tend to see these changes as developments or improvements, so that it is assumed that we are dealing with progressively better accounts of the nature of intelligence.

Thus Guildford's multi-factorial model of intelligence, which, as set forth in 1967, contains no fewer than 120 mental factors, would be popularly supposed to be an improvement on Thurstone's (1931) factor analysis, which in turn would be seen as a development of Spearman's (1904) two-factor theory of intelligence.[5] And again, a common presumption would be that Guildford's subsequent (1982) model involving 150 distinct abilities represents a refinement and advance on his earlier account.[6] However, it is by no means the case that more recent theories are necessarily superior to, or indeed as good as, earlier ones. Clarifying concepts is not a business that lends itself to progressive improvement as readily as perhaps scientific discovery does. We must beware of confusing specificity with clarity, and assuming that a longer, more specific list of aspects necessarily makes for a clearer concept of intelligence, or that either specificity or clarity alone can ensure coherence and plausibility. Thus it would be a mistake to consider psychology's contribution to the debate by focusing on current theory and research: with regard to the concept itself there is no particular reason to assume that today's view is superior to yesterday's, just as there is no particular reason to assume that any philosopher today has anything more illuminating to say about the concept of friendship than Aristotle had. (They may have, but if they do it will only marginally be because they come later in time and can profit from the work of predecessors. Science tends to be progressive and accumulative because we find out more and more about the functioning of an element. But trying to formulate an understanding of the nature of a concept, particularly of an abstract idea, is not primarily a matter of finding out more about it.) It is, besides, instructive to consider a number of varied responses to the question of what intelligence is, provided by psychologists over the years.

In 1923, Boring asserted that 'intelligence is what the tests test'.[7] This uncompromising statement, ambiguous as it is, should probably not be interpreted as a definition. That is to say, it does not mean 'when I call a person intelligent, I am saying that they do well on intelligence tests'. Such a view would be open to the objection that it is pretty obviously not what people typically mean when they ascribe intelligence to someone. A more plausible interpretation is that Boring meant 'while I am not offering a definition, let alone an analysis, of intelligence, I maintain that success in such tests is closely related to intelligent behaviour, and, for practical purposes, we psychologists should agree to equate the two'. In other words it amounts to an operational definition, designed to achieve some clarity and unanimity concerning what they are researching into. But how could one substantiate a claim about the relationship between performance on such tests and intelligence in the absence of some (other) satisfactory understanding of the latter notion? How could I know, to take an analogy, that a certain drug cured cancer (never mind how), if I didn't have a clear idea of what cancer was? And what is the sense in equating test performance and intelligence, even for operational purposes, when at best we claim a correlation between the two. Whatever Boring's actual intentions here (and I do not see him as confused or stupid, so much as dangerously misleading), there can be little doubt that for a long time many people have proceeded as if he had said, and correctly at that, that an intelligent person is one and the same thing as a person who performs well on a certain kind of test. We are of course at liberty to assert boldly that this is what we choose to mean by intelligence, but in so doing we raise the questions of why we are proffering a definition that does not accord in any way with normal assumptions about the concept, hazy as they may be, and why anybody should particularly value intelligence in this sense.

In 1958 Wechsler defined intelligence as 'the global and aggregate capacity of an individual to think rationally, to act purposefully and to deal effectively with his environment'.[8] There are features of this definition that make it a distinct improvement on those we have so far considered, notwithstanding the fact that it was formulated earlier than two of them. The question of what exactly is meant by a capacity, whether it is general, whether it is presumed to be innate or acquired, and indeed whether there is one, remains. But there is something to be said for the view that what we mean by calling someone intelligent is essentially that they think rationally; specific reference to purposive activity is also to be welcomed (and reminds us that the question of which species of animal have intelligence needs to be addressed in terms of whether they can be said to act with purpose, rather than simply to do things that happen to serve a purpose), and the inclusion of reference to coping with one's environment introduces a potentially important distinction between theoretical and practical intelligence. For all that, analysis would require us to push this account considerably further: does the intelligent person necessarily think rationally in all spheres? What more precisely constitutes thinking rationally? How does one distinguish between acting purposefully and acting to good purpose? And what is meant by being able to 'deal effectively' with the environment? All such questions would need to be answered before one could make uncontroversial use of this definition, and one may assert very simply that it is the fact that they were not that makes the tests of intelligence devised by Wechsler very questionable (regardless of their technical quality and the fact that they are still in use).

In 1904 Spearman had advanced the thesis that any mental task involves two distinct factors: a general factor *(g)* and a specific factor *(s)* such as verbal, arithmetic, or musical ability.[9] He further argued that the *g* factor could be broken down into various more specific mental functions such as the ability to grasp relationships, to abstract, or to solve problems. These general abilities he saw as characteristics of intelligence, to be contrasted with related but distinct characteristics such as rote memory and sensory processes. Taken as a theoretical construct, albeit of an unrealistically schematic kind (can arithmetical ability be entirely divorced from verbal ability? Is the ability to grasp relationships entirely distinct from the ability to solve problems?), this is not altogether unreasonable. Although we do not know that there is some general ability, still less whether it is an innate quality in the individual, it is *prima facie* an advance (though note the date of Spearman's contribution) to recognize that, whether we call it part of intelligence or not, mental activity will always involve some specific ability such as arithmetical or musical. Even if intelligence were to be defined in purely generic terms, evidence of intelligence would have to emerge in some particular context: it would be logically impossible to display one's ability to solve problems, for example, without solving some arithmetic, musical, or other specific kind of problem. Furthermore, to anticipate an important theme, even if that were not the case, there is the question of whether we should value or care about a generic intelligence, as opposed to intelligence displayed in specific areas.

Beyond that, however, the major point to be made is that whether intelligence is or is not to be characterized in some such terms is not an empirical issue, and cannot ultimately be resolved by any amount of empirical study based on this hypothesis. Memory, for example, is theoretically distinguishable from verbal skills (though one may wonder how they could be entirely divorced in practice); but whether we regard the former as part of the concept of intelligence remains a philosophical question that requires judgement and a reflective decision, and can only be decided by asking questions such as whether we should wish to regard a person who could not remember anything as intelligent, or whether it makes sense to imagine a person without memory being able to engage in other mental activities. In short, Spearman offers us the outline of a way of conceiving of intelligence, but that outline is in need of considerable further elucidation, is supported by no reasoning or argument, and at least in some respects (e.g., the idea that one could have a general ability of grasping relationships, as opposed to the ability to grasp certain kinds of relationship in certain contexts) is highly questionable.

Hebb's 1966 distinction between what he calls Intelligence A and Intelligence B is instructive. Intelligence A is the 'innate potential for cognitive development'; Intelligence B is 'a general or average level of development of ability to perceive, to learn, to solve problems, to think, to adapt'.[10] The distinction explicitly draws attention to a tension that we have already noted implicitly between the idea of some innate capacity and the developed state of that capacity. It is certainly very important, whether we are talking about the value of intelligence or researching into ways to assess or develop it, to know which we are talking about. A problem remains for Intelligence A in that whether, to what extent, and in what sense it exists remains conjectural and must continue to do so, since, by definition, one cannot establish the existence of a potential in its unrealized form. Only people who display Intelligence B can reasonably be said to have certainly possessed Intelligence A. But that leaves unanswered the question of whether in saying that such people had Intelligence A we are saying that their genetic inheritance was such as to allow them to develop Intelligence B, or that they acquired Intelligence B through learning and other environmental factors.

Two points are worth stressing about this selection of psychological definitions of intelligence. First, as has been pointed out, one cannot reasonably see them as representing a historical line of increasingly refined and plausible definitions. This is not surprising if we bear in mind that they are not (and necessarily are not) the product of empirical research, but are theoretical constructs, the quality of which depends primarily on the insight and ability of the individual in question to engage in conceptual analysis, rather than on increased data relating to so-called intelligent behaviour. The second point, which is closely linked to the first, is that the weakness of all the definitions referred to is that none of them involves an attempt to thoroughly explore and understand what is meant by the idea of intelligence. In varying degree, they are superficial characterizations that do no more than indicate some broad, contentious, and unargued for assumptions. They are either broad and vague definitions of the dictionary type, which do no more than outline what it is we are referring to, or they involve questionable theories about how intelligence functions, or both.

As Vernon pointed out in 1969, some psychologists assume in their definitions that intelligence is or involves a genetic capacity, others that it is to be identified with some kind of performance on certain tests, and others that it is identifiable with certain observed behaviours.[11] Provided that we are aware of which kind of view is operative in any case, we may learn something useful about intelligence in the sense in question. For example, we might learn that good performance on a certain kind of test correlates highly with certain other achievements, or that certain kinds of behaviour are promoted by certain kinds of teaching practice. In itself such knowledge may be useful and this kind of research therefore regarded as entirely reasonable; but whether it is telling us anything about intelligence is an entirely different question, to answer which there is no alternative to engaging directly in analysis without concern for operational restraints. If anybody is tempted to say, 'Well, the question of what intelligence is in some abstract sense is not important compared with finding out something concrete about "intelligence" defined in some manageable way', the sharp retort should be, 'But why should we care about intelligence defined in some manageable way, if it is not in fact intelligence? Call it what you will, why should we care about the individual's ability to perform well on certain standardized tests? What does it matter if people can perform certain observable behaviours?' There may of course be convincing answers to these questions. Perhaps the behaviours that define intelligence for a particular researcher are educationally very important, or perhaps the point is that they correlate significantly with other behaviours that have value. Perhaps. But such questions are typically not even raised, let alone answered. It is not the case, for instance, that anyone has put up a convincing argument for the inherent value of performing well on a standardized achievement test, nor is there a great deal of evidence that people who do well on them necessarily do well in other important educational respects. The main reason why people unreflectively take them seriously is that they are taken to be some kind of index of intelligence in a desirable sense. But that is precisely what has not been shown.

The basic problem can be illustrated by reference to Jensen's (1986) research on reaction time.[12] Working on the hypothesis that speed of mental processing (or simply thinking) is or might be a major factor in superior intelligence, Jensen devised a test, which required no particular knowledge or physical skills, to assess the speed of the subject's reaction to a stimulus or cue. Essentially, the speed with which the subject removed a finger from a button when a light came on beside another button was tested. We are told that the research showed that there was a negative correlation between the reaction time and intelligence as measured by standardized tests.

Now, assuming that the research itself was not flawed in some technical sense, such as that unbeknownst to us the subjects had arthritic hands, what can we reasonably conclude from this experiment? The unwary will conclude that speed is not a factor in intelligence. The slightly more sophisticated might recognize the alternative possibility that standardized tests do not measure intelligence, and that therefore speed has not been shown to be an irrelevant factor. But the empirical research in itself does not help us at all in deciding between these or various other options. The question of whether speed in thinking is an aspect of intelligence is a question that can only be answered by thinking about the concept, by reflection on what we mean, by argument about the kind of thinking that we presume to dignify with the title of 'intelligent'.

To be specific, in this case there are a number of quite different things we might say. We could argue that speed *is* an essential part of what we mean by intelligence, but it is speed in dealing with argument, not merely speed of reaction to a stimulus. We could argue that the ability to perform well on a standardized achievement test is neither what we mean by intelligence nor has been shown to have any obvious connection with what we mean, and therefore speed has not been shown to be irrelevant. We cannot legitimately conclude that, in so far as it is empirically the case that speed of reaction of this type and performance on a standardized test of this type are not related, intelligence cannot be defined in terms of both. For it might be the case that it is to be defined in terms of both, but unfortunately none of the subjects was in fact intelligent. In short, without prior agreement on a reasonably full characterization of intelligence, nothing at all can be concluded about intelligence from this or any similar kind of empirical research. We can conclude only that speed of manual response to a visual signal of a very simplistic type does not necessarily go hand in hand with good performance on a test such as an IQ test. Put in this way, we are surely at least tempted to respond by asking, 'so what?'. Why should we care about either? Why should we care about whether and to what extent they are related? Why should we value either ability? What has either of them got to do with the valued quality of intelligence?

The fact is that psychologists, *qua* psychologists, are trying to answer empirical, contingent, questions about intelligence, rather than to determine what it is or what constitutes or counts as intelligence. Their job is to discover what they can about what happens to be or not be the case about intelligent people, other than the fact that they are intelligent. Do they sleep well, are they happy, do they do well in school, do they have successful careers, do they react quickly to physical stimuli; and so forth. But it makes no sense to ask such questions about intelligent people, if you don't have a clear idea of what is meant by an intelligent person. In practical terms, to allow others to make sense of and judge your research for themselves, this involves articulating that conception for public scrutiny, the more clearly and the more fully, the better. Nor, as we have seen *(pp. 3 - 15)*, can the empirical process be used directly to refine or increase our understanding of the meaning of the concept, although sometimes empirical data may provide stimulating food for thought: for if we define intelligence as *A* and attempt to establish that it must in fact be defined as *A* and *B*, since they are invariably found together, it is still a matter of decision as to whether we should conclude that intelligence always goes hand in hand with *B*, or that it should be defined in terms of both *A* and *B*. When, as in this case, the correlation is negative, the research is even less helpful, for the reason given: we can conclude either that *A* and *B* should not both be part of the definition of intelligence, since they are not significantly found together, or that they should be, and the fact is that there are few, if any, truly intelligent people. Deciding which way to go has nothing to do with the empirical research.

Presumably because at some level this point is recognized, researchers do seek to make it clear what they take intelligence to be. The problem is that in the vast majority of cases the working definitions provided are insufficiently clear or fully articulated, and in many cases, such as those considered, they are at best contentious and at worst inadequate.

So far as educationalists, including educational psychologists, are concerned, there is a prior question of supreme importance. Not only do we need a clearly articulated conception of intelligence to make sense of empirical research, we also need a conception that has plausibility in terms of educational significance. As educators, we are interested in intelligence because we believe that it is a concept of central importance in education. It is therefore important that our definition should be in terms that have some educational value. A hostile critic would say that, regardless of other weaknesses, a good number of working definitions of intelligence in psychology are couched in terms that represent nothing of educational interest to us. Thus, an objection to a definition in terms of performance on standardized tests might be, not so much that it is not actually what most people mean by intelligence, as that we do not see any inherent value in such an ability, call it what you will. A fairer-minded individual might prefer to put the point this way: while it is very interesting to have evidence to the effect that speed of reaction in a certain kind of test does not correlate significantly with good performance on a certain kind of standardized test, a far more important educational question is whether either of them matters.

Intelligence Testing

This brings us directly to the substantive question of the value of standardized tests of intelligence. Do they involve an implicit definition of intelligence, or are they meant to be instruments for locating intelligence, defined in some other way? If the former, do we have any reason to care about intelligence in this sense? If the latter, has any argument been produced for supposing that they do relate to intelligence in some way? (It is quite often maintained that such tests have lost their credibility today, and individual psychologists have certainly been known to regard them with a certain amount of disdain. None the less, they continue to be widely used in school districts, they continue to play an integral part in much research, and the logic of intelligence testing is the same as the logic of any standardized tests such as those that are still widely endorsed in research into, for example, giftedness, creativity, and critical thinking.)

An intelligence test, whatever its precise form, seeks to establish the level of intelligence of individuals by requiring them to perform a series of tasks. (The difference between individual and group tests is of no relevance to us here, nor are technical questions about modes of scoring, and so on.) Tasks may include such things as providing definitions of words, engaging in simple reasoning, completing jigsaw-type puzzles, showing general knowledge, pointing out pictures that correspond to words, drawing something such as 'the best man possible',[13] completing series, pointing out similarities, or arranging pictures to tell a story.

The nature of all such tasks, the crucial feature of which is that they should involve as little reliance on acquired bodies of knowledge and experience as possible, is easily explained and immediately throws into relief a crucially begged question. The idea is that we are testing some general innate capacity which in so far as individuals have it, will enable them to cope intelligently with argument and experience. It is therefore necessary to divorce the test from things that have to be learned or are otherwise the product of experience rather than basic intelligence. We cannot test by means of inquiring into the individual's capacity to deal with, say, a historical argument, a discussion about abortion, or a theory of aesthetic value, since it will be widely agreed that one's capacity in such cases will be to a large extent governed by what one has studied and learned. Straight away, we realize that this approach to testing intelligence presupposes that there is such a thing as a general capacity that can be divorced, both theoretically and practically, from acquired understanding. Unfortunately, no argument has ever been produced to establish the plausibility of this highly contentious and problematic assumption.

It sounds well enough, and might be thought to gain credibility from the undisputed facts that interference with particular parts of the brain can affect the capacity to perform particular kinds of mental operation, that people generally do presume that intelligence is a general capacity to process information and knowledge which is to be distinguished from what they learn, and that it is a matter of common experience that certain people (whom we call intelligent) tend to be able to deal intelligently with a variety of issues. But none of this actually proves anything, and there is a rather more plausible account of the concept of intelligence that accounts for these points equally well or better.

It is true that different parts of the brain are to be associated with the capacity to perform various different kinds of mental activity. The details need not concern us here: it is enough to know that if the brain is impaired by drugs or physical damage the individual ceases to be able to perform intelligently, and that, if some specific intrusion is made, say a frontal lobotomy, some mental operations are affected and not others. To know this is to know that the normal functioning of the brain is a necessary prerequisite of intelligent performance. It does not necessarily lead to the conclusion that various parts of the brain are to be identified with various general capacities such as the capacity to spot relationships, to solve problems, or to detect logical sequences.

The fact that people may often presume that there is some general capacity to which we refer when we talk of intelligence is neither surprising nor compelling. It is not surprising, partly because for many years now the so-called experts have been promulgating this idea, and partly because it is a much more long-standing historical fact that people, rightly or wrongly, tend to reify or see abstract concepts in concrete terms. (The soul, for example, has passed from being conceived of as a physical entity, through being conceived of as a metaphysical abstraction, to being, to some, a purely fictional entity.) It is not compelling, because people may be wrong. The truth of a matter is not determined by a head count of those in agreement.

The third point cuts both ways: yes, by and large intelligent people do not confine their intelligence to one sphere. But, on the other hand, were there ever intelligent people who could literally turn their hand to anything? Even Leonardo da Vinci is not known to have been particularly intelligent in respect of his private life or politics. Most intelligent people of our acquaintance even more obviously have limits on the areas in which they are able to display intelligence.

Now, there is a reason why this last point is so. Superficially one might say, indeed almost everybody would say, that, however intelligent da Vinci is, he cannot proceed intelligently in areas of which he is ignorant. Thus, it will generally be conceded that, even if there is such a thing as a general intelligence, to proceed intelligently, and still more obviously to be recognized as intelligent, one will need to know certain things. To be an intelligent historian or car salesperson one will need, in addition to having the putative quality of intelligence, to understand history or the car market. But now the question arises of what one could possibly mean by the capacity to proceed intelligently divorced from any particular context. It is not that one needs information and understanding *in addition to* the general capacity in order to function, but rather that the capacity does not make sense, it is inconceivable, except in some context, however trivial. How could I meaningfully be said to have the capacity to spot relationships, if there are not any relationships of a particular kind that I can spot? And if it is agreed that what is actually referred to by the phrase 'a general capacity to spot relationships' is a 'capacity to spot some specific relationships that do not depend upon any obvious complex bodies of understanding', then it should become immediately apparent that a general capacity in this sense is not necessarily of much value in itself.

That we are not in fact dealing with a mysterious general capacity divorced from any context is shown by the history of IQ testing and, in particular, of criticism levelled against it. Many years ago critics began to point out that the claim of such tests to be objective in the sense of culturally neutral and unrelated to people's upbringing and education was untenable. Even the simplest of items presupposes some knowledge that has been acquired and is to some extent culturally specific. Hence in the early days the objection was raised that tests discriminated against certain groups such as American blacks. While various particular problems may have been ironed out, the fact remains that the ability to complete the series 4:8:16:32, to recognize the odd one out in lemon, pear, fig, potato, to draw a good picture of a man, or to recognize what is wrong in a picture of two people sitting in deck chairs in the rain, are all to some extent dependent on what one has learned, which in turn will in some cases be affected by the environment in which one grew up. The idea that ability at such tasks is exclusively the product of one's genetic inheritance is absurd (which is not to say that genetic factors may not play a part in determining one's intelligence), and the further idea that such ability betokens one's ability to live one's life intelligently or to become an intelligent historian could only be seriously maintained if there were to be clear evidence (which there is not) that success in test performance correlates positively with the latter.[14]

It seems then, that the idea of intelligence divorced from any content is unintelligible and that actual intelligence tests are not divorced from content. However, they tend to involve a content that, on the one hand, is to some extent bound to a particular culture, and, on the other, as a result of the impossible quest to denude it of contextual knowledge, is by and large relatively trivial. Thus, one might say, the only real difference between an IQ test and an essay or an examination of a more traditional and academic type, is that the former tests one's ability to perform intellectual tasks in a trivial context, the latter in a more complex context. The questions one would naturally want to raise, therefore, are, first, why should we regard these as tests of intelligence rather than as tests of the ability to complete this numerical series, that puzzle, and so on? Second, why should we care about these abilities? And third, do they have any predictive value in respect of matters of educational importance?

The answer to the first question appears to be that there is no good reason to regard them as tests of intelligence. They test a number of particular skills that do not on the face of it recommend themselves as an account of intelligence. When I classify da Vinci as intelligent I do not mean that I have reason to believe he could perform well on such a test. It is difficult also to answer the second question in any positive fashion, unless we can relate it to the third question. That is to say, whether this is what some people mean by intelligence or not, I have no interest in the child's ability to perform such tasks *per se*. I do not value ability in these respects any more than I value the ability to do crossword puzzles, play Scrabble, win Trivial Pursuits, do jigsaws, or guess who did it in a detective story. (I should perhaps indicate that I am not against such things; I do not deride them. I merely observe that as an educationalist I have my sights on something rather different.)

So a lot comes to hinge upon the question of what positive correlation there may be between good performance on these tests and other performances that we do see reason to value. Unfortunately, the answer is disappointing to say the least. For it turns out that there is no evidence of a strong link between IQ and such things as subsequent academic success, career progress, or, most important, intelligence conceived of in the way that I shall outline in the next chapter.

It must be admitted that it is sometimes maintained that, on the contrary, IQ is closely related to subsequent academic success, and the basic fact of a substantial positive correlation between intelligence test score and school achievement could not be appropriately challenged in the context of a book such as this. But we need to remember, first, that labelling an individual as one with a high IQ, or conversely a low IQ, is likely to have a self-fulfilling effect; second, that there is a considerable degree of similarity between some of the items on an intelligence test and some tests of school achievement (and note in this respect that the correlation is highest where the similarity is most marked - success in intelligence tests correlates particularly highly with success in subjects involving verbal and numerical skills, which are, after all, the kinds of skill most commonly drawn upon in intelligence testing); and third, that the correlation is much lower than that between previous and subsequent achievement, so that an intelligence test would be a worse predictor of future mathematical ability, or whatever, than a mathematics test would be. Putting all this together, it seems at least questionable whether we should conclude that we have here an instrument that we should rely on to make judgements about individuals' future chances of academic success. Much more importantly, it is obvious that the relevance of this type of test diminishes proportionately to the extent that our view of ultimate academic success is different in kind from the type of ability assessed by such tests. That is primarily why I said above that there was 'no evidence of a strong link between IQ and subsequent academic success'. There is no evidence of a strong link between IQ and academic success in any sense other than that measured by standardized tests.

Correlations with subsequent job success are low. While this can to some extent be explained away (e.g., Gage and Berliner, 'this does not mean that IQ is unimportant. It simply means that many other factors also determine job success'[15]), it doesn't alter the fact that no reason to administer such tests is to be found here. Whatever the reason, we are being told unambiguously that these are not useful instruments for attempting to predict future success. But our major concern should be to point out that to consider the value of IQ tests by reference to how well they predict subsequent performance on more specific but none the less similar achievement tests is to render the whole exercise somewhat circular. What the tests actually test, I have argued, is pretty trivial. However, if the tests turn out to be useful predictors of something useful, they may have some value. But what they predict is really nothing more than more sophisticated versions of the same trivia. They may predict success on other relatively sterile achievement tests, but there is no evidence at all that they can predict anything about genuine educational success, which is to say about such things as people's ability to study science, theology, history, or literature with enthusiasm, understanding, and profit at the tertiary level. Once again it is conceptual confusion that causes the problem. Intelligence testing began without an adequate conception of intelligence and continues without an adequate conception of education.

What, then, is the overall message to be taken from this review of psychology and intelligence? That at best psychologists are advancing knowledge of intrinsic interest but no obvious educational importance; at worst they are misleading and damaging the chances of coherent educational research and discourse. There is, of course, a real question to be asked about the physiological basis of intelligence. And, if it so happened that we could establish that one's ability to conduct oneself intelligently through life depended entirely on the state of one's brain at birth, it would have very important, if somewhat frightening, repercussions. But this, although it is implied by much, particularly early, work in the field, remains at the level of a fairly implausible hypothesis. Research has not produced any grounds for advancing beyond the Platonic thesis formulated 2,500 years ago, which is well expressed in Stern's contemporary rubber band analogy: this suggests that different individuals are born with different potential (exemplified by the length of the rubber band), but that a great deal depends upon what is done with that individual (that is, how far the band is stretched); and, of course, the fact is that some smaller rubber bands may be stretched to a greater extent than some bigger ones.[16] One of the functions of the school, one might say, is to stretch rubber bands. Too much research and educational practice is focused on trying to classify rubber bands by size. Far more important, even if we knew more than we do about sizing rubber bands, is to investigate ways of stretching them.

That being the case, it would seem far more important to establish what we want to achieve with the student's intellect, and to test the value of our teaching and our educational programme in terms of what we are trying to achieve, than to seek to estimate an alleged innate quality. An overemphasis on the psychological approach could, if we are not careful, lead us to assume that the mind is a certain kind of entity, which it is not, that certain kinds of specific skills are important, which they are not, and that there are certain general abilities divorced from any context, which there are not and cannot be.

Notes and references

1. See Barrow, R., (1990), *Understanding Skills: Thinking, feeling and caring*, London, Ontario: Althouse Press.
2. Gage, N.L. and Berliner, D.C., (1979), *Educational Psychology*, 2nd edn, Chicago: Rand McNally, p. 71.
3. Lefrancois, G.R., (1988), *Psychology for Teaching*, 6th edn, Belmont, Cal: Wadsworth, p. 208.
4. Harré, R. and Lamb, R., (1986), *The Dictionary of Developmental and Educational Psychology*, Cambridge, Mass: MIT Press, p. 124.
5. Guildford, J.P., (1967), *The Nature of Human Intelligence*, New York: McGraw Hill; Thurstone, L.L., (1931), 'Multiple factor analysis', *Psychological Review*, 38, 406 - 27; Spearman, C.E., (1904), 'General intelligence objectively determined and measured', *American Journal of Psychology*, 15, 201 - 93.
6. Guildford, J.P., (1982), 'Cognitive psychology's ambiguities; Some suggested remedies', *Psychological Review*, 89, 48 - 9.
7. Boring, E.G., (1923), 'Intelligence as the tests test it', *New Republic*, 35, 35 - 7.
8. Wechsler, D., (1958), *The Measurement and Appraisal of Adult Intelligence*, 4th edn, Baltimore: Williams and Wilkins, p. 7.
9. Spearman, C.E., (1904), op. cit.
10. Hebb, D.O., (1966), *A Textbook of Psychology*, 2nd edn, Philadelphia: W.B. Saunders, p. 332.
11. Vernon, P.E., (1969), *Intelligence and Cultural Environment*, London: Methuen.
12. Jensen, A.R., (1986), 'Intelligence: definition, measurement and future research', in Sternberg, R.J., and Detterman, D.K., (eds), *What is Intelligence?* Norwood, N.J.: Ablex.
13. This more than usually curious item was initially developed in Goodenough, F., (1926), *Measurement of Intelligence by Drawings*, New York: Harcourt, Brace and World.
14. Sharon Bailin suggests that I am not giving enough weight to the idea of a certain capacity (say, to spot relationships) being generalizable across contexts. But I maintain that this does not make sense, unless interpreted as either a capacity to spot relationships in various non-complex situations or the capacity to spot relationships in one (or more) substantive areas, which would presuppose understanding in those areas. My fundamental reason for maintaining this is that the nature of relationships (i.e., what constitutes a relationship) will necessarily vary from field to field, and therefore understanding of a particular field is logically required to make sense of the idea of spotting relationships in that field. E.g., I cannot spot relationships in physics or contemporary pop groups because I know little about either, not because I am relatively lacking in some general capacity. Of course I do not dispute that some formal qualities are common to many contexts. Thus, 'spotting relationships' may well be a necessary part of intelligent performance in any context. (But note my use of the phrase 'common to' in preference to 'transferable' or 'generalizable', and note that this in no way contradicts what has been said before!) It is also readily conceded that a person may have a disposition to, e.g., look for relationships, which by definition means that he is inclined to do so in a wide variety of contexts.
15. Gage, N.L. and Berliner, D.C., (1979), op. cit., p. 82.
16. Cited without reference in Lefrancois, G.R., (1988), *Psychology for Teaching*, 6th edn, Belmont, Cal.: Wadsworth.

3. Philosophy and Intelligence

Criteria for Adequate Analysis

In the preceding pages I have distinguished between definition and analysis, and argued that it is the latter that is urgently required: we need to get a clear and fully articulated understanding of what we mean by intelligence - of what criteria have to be met for someone to count as an intelligent person - partly to be able to make better sense of research in the field, but mainly because as educators we need a clear idea of what we are aiming at. Without such an analysis we have no way of judging our progress and no way of ordering our activity. We cannot make reasonable judgements about people's intelligence, we cannot conduct meaningful research into contingent questions such as how it is distributed through the population, and we cannot answer questions such as whether it can be developed, whether it is innate or the product of environment, or what the appropriate steps to foster it may be. The problem with much psychological research in the area is that it has settled for definitions (rather than analysis) which in various ways are ambiguous or superficial, avoid or beg important questions, and are of no obvious educational value. It is not necessary to argue that they are false or incorrect definitions: the point is that they are inadequate for our purposes.

At this point more needs to be said about the nature of analysis itself. There is a school of thought, allegedly stemming from Plato, that sees concepts as in some way given, and the philosopher's task as capturing a concept and revealing its actual essence. According to this view the task of analysis is analogous to the task of the lepidopterist. The latter captures a butterfly that has an independent existence and specific features or characteristics: the lepidopterist pins it down, studies it, and describes its characteristics. In the same way, the philosopher, metaphorically speaking, brings the concept of justice or education down to earth, dissects it, and reveals its actual properties. The implication of this view is clearly that there is a true or correct answer to a question such as, 'What is justice?'

At the other extreme is the view that there is no such thing as the true meaning of a concept. The concept of justice is what we make it, and hence in the

37

normal order of things there will be historical developments in the life of a concept, and competing definitions. Justice will not necessarily be the same thing for a classical Greek, a contemporary Turk, or, indeed, for you or me. In its extreme form this view may lead some to the conclusion that there is no given and permanent meaning to a concept: everything is as you see it. Between these two extremes lie a number of varied positions, both in respect of the extent to which a concept is thought to have some identity of its own (such as the extent to which justice is thought to have some essential meaning, regardless of what people may think about it), and in respect of the means thought appropriate to trying to establish the meaning of a concept.

The position assumed here is that while one is restricted in what one can reasonably say about a concept both by the demands of logic and by the facts of the world, as we understand them at any given time, there is always an element of decision-making or judgement in analysis, and in the case of relatively complex and abstract concepts that element looms large.

It is important here to distinguish between a word and a concept. The word 'education', for example, will be defined in any English language dictionary in terms that have something to do with upbringing, learning, and knowledge. If, therefore, one defines education as 'a substance separated unchanged from another substance', one may reasonably be told that one has simply made a mistake, confusing the word 'educt' with the word 'education'. But this is a verbal rather than a conceptual mistake. The conceptual issue does not arise until we have got to the point of using the appropriate word and begun to ask questions about the idea behind it, such as what kind of upbringing or learning constitutes education. It is in pursuing that kind of question, I am arguing, that there are both restraints on what one can reasonably say, and yet a degree of judgement required.

Thus, even when dealing with the concept of something physical and relatively straightforward, such as a bear, while one is not at liberty to argue that bears have five legs and can run at 200 mph (since the fact of the matter is that the creatures we refer to as 'bears' don't have these characteristics), nor to make self-contradictory or incoherent claims, none the less judgement may be called for. Suppose, for example, we come across a new species that does have five legs and can run at 200 mph but is otherwise like traditional bears. Whether we classify this as a species of bear, with unusual characteristics, or as a new species, is surely a matter of choice or decision. The suggestion that it either is or is not a bear, and that we must find out empirically which it is, does not seem to make sense. It is what it is. We have to use our judgement as to how to classify it. Indeed, this appears to be part of the reason that zoologists are divided as to whether to classify the panda as a bear. It is not lack of empirical knowledge that keeps the matter open to debate, but the fact that no amount of empirical knowledge can settle the issue: we have to decide whether or not to modify our conception of bear to allow for pandas. This element of decision-making, however, is not entirely arbitrary. It will be governed by rational considerations such as consideration of the extent of difference between pandas and other bears, the nature of the difference, and the utility of deciding one way or the other.

When we turn to more abstract concepts such as justice and education the role of judgement naturally increases, since the restraints of empirical fact are fewer. Bears, if we forget about pandas, do clearly have certain characteristics rather than others. Because we are dealing with a physical creature, the broad boundaries of the concept are not contentious: once we have decided to subdivide the animal kingdom into visibly distinct species, to a very large extent what counts as being a bear is given in nature. The case is very different with a concept such as education. Of course there are still some restraints on what we can reasonably say. Starting at the verbal level, as already noted, if we are trying to get to grips with the idea behind the word, we are entitled at the outset to ignore those who simply seem to be using the wrong word, confusing, for example, 'education' with 'love'. But, beyond that point the fact of the matter is that, even if we understand that 'education' means broadly something like 'instruction' or 'upbringing', the types of activity that have gone and do go on in the name of education vary considerably, different people do have very different ideas of what kinds of upbringing and instruction count as education. We therefore cannot proceed by subjecting undisputed instances of education to closer scrutiny, as we can with bears, since part of what is disputed is which instances are genuine instances of education. Thus judgement and reasoning are required rather than mere observation and empirical data. In particular, in this case, value judgements have to be made, since education is a normative concept. That is to say, education is presumed to be a desirable thing and therefore our view of what it involves will necessarily include reference to our view of what kind of upbringing is to be valued. Our conception of education has to be formulated in the light of consideration of what we believe to be reasonable, possible, and desirable in respect of the upbringing of children, as well as, more generally, consideration of what distinctions we want to draw between education and similar but distinguishable concepts such as socialization, training, and indoctrination. All of this requires that we make choices and decisions rather than merely reveal or discover undisputed characteristics of a given thing.

Recognizing the fact that a crucial part of conceptual analysis is a matter of making a decision or choice, however, emphatically does not mean that anything goes, or that it is a matter of arbitrary preference whether one defines a term in this way or that. Apart from the constraints of the way things are, already referred to, there are the constraints of reason which operate even when we are dealing with extremely abstract and contentious concepts. These constraints may conveniently be categorized in terms of the Four Cs: clarity, coherence, completeness, and compatibility.

Clarity is an obvious desideratum, though not perhaps as evident in practice as it ought to be. Any adequate attempt to analyse a concept must be couched in terms that are themselves clear, rather than opaque, obscure, ambiguous, or arcane. To be told that creativity is to be defined as 'the capacity to evoke effective surprise' is inadequate on this criterion alone, since, though in this particular case the individual words are not obscure, exactly what is meant by the definition as a whole is remarkably unclear: what is meant by 'effective surprise' is vague, as is the question of in whom the surprise needs to be evoked (the agent, discriminating judges, anyone?). But clarity alone is not enough. It is possible to be clear but incoherent, most obviously by being contradictory or inconsistent. An adequate account of what it is to be creative, to be educated, to be just, or to be intelligent, must obviously be presented in terms that are both clear and internally consistent or coherent.

So much would be generally admitted, at least in principle. The other two criteria need emphasizing because they are less widely recognized. One of the main tests of the adequacy of an attempt at analysis is the degree of its completeness. One cannot indicate the appropriate degree of completeness in quantitative terms - it is not a matter of saying 'all concepts should be analysed in ten to fifteen lines'. How full an analysis is required for completeness will depend upon the nature and complexity of the individual concept. For example, to say that a bachelor is an unmarried male is entirely adequate, whereas to say that an intelligent person is one who has understanding is not. To appreciate why the former is adequate and the latter is not is once again a matter of judgement, but the explanation of the difference is to be found in the fact that the notion of 'an unmarried male' is clear and unproblematic, whereas the notion of 'understanding' requires further elaboration: what constitutes understanding? does any kind of understanding count? and so forth. The criterion of completeness requires us to push our analysis as far as we can, to expand on the various elements in our definition to the point at which everything is clear and unproblematic.

The criterion of compatibility plays a major part in preventing us from producing technically adequate analyses that are none the less of little practical value because they are highly idiosyncratic. It would be possible to produce an analysis of education that started from the broad and accepted dictionary definition of the word as 'the act or process of imparting knowledge', that was couched in clear and coherent terms, and that was reasonably complete, but that none the less seemed quite bizarre to others. But, if the analysis is to be adequate, all the steps along the way must also be consistent or compatible with other things that we know or believe. In this case, whatever we say in attempting to give a fuller account of the process in question must be circumscribed by such empirical knowledge as we have of various techniques for imparting knowledge and our beliefs about them (for example, some techniques don't work, some are immoral) and by our understanding of the nature of knowledge. Because we can only do one thing at a time, because we cannot analyse a concept in a vacuum, and because as a matter of fact we have a vast array of shared knowledge and agreed concepts, when it gets down to it, if we do the job properly, we find that many *prima facie* conceptual disagreements cannot sincerely be maintained. It turns out that a given account of what it is to be educated is at some point, in some respect, simply incompatible with other facts, beliefs, or values to which we are committed.

It cannot be overemphasized that the restraints set upon us by verbal convention, by the facts of the world, and by the criteria of clarity, coherence, completeness, and compatibility, bring a considerable degree of objectivity and rationality to the business of analysis. It involves a fundamental misunderstanding to think that one may coherently define a concept in any way that one chooses, and that consequently there are no grounds for objecting to a given conception. However, that having been said, it does remain the case that one cannot conclusively demonstrate that to be educated means such and such, nor prove it either empirically or by strict logic. One has to reason and convince.

The objection to all the psychological definitions referred to above can now be put more succinctly and precisely: to varying degrees, some of them lacked clarity and had an element of incoherence. They were all woefully incomplete. They were all almost certainly inadequate on the criterion of compatibility, though whether and in what ways that was in fact the case in each instance cannot easily be said, since they all fail completely to explain and give reasons for accepting the assumptions implicit in them. To take but one example, apart from other shortcomings, a definition of intelligence in terms of a general ability presupposes that the idea of general abilities, divorced from specific contexts, makes sense. If it does not, then such an analysis is incompatible with this awkward fact. But such analyses have been produced without even going into the question of whether the idea makes sense.

Intelligence as a Process

In now seeking to elaborate an adequate conception of intelligence, I start with
four fairly uncontroversial assumptions. First, that intelligence is something we
value (and therefore our analysis must ultimately be in terms of things that we do
indeed value). Secondly, that, so far as education goes, our interest is in
capitalizing on intelligence. What this means in practice will depend upon what
kind of thing we finally take intelligence to be, but amongst things that it might
mean are that we want to make accurate estimates of individuals' intelligence or
that we want to develop their intelligence. The former would be all that we
could do, if it were to turn out that we mean by intelligence a capacity that is both
innate and fixed, so that we could no more change people's intelligence than the
colour of their eyes, whereas the latter, if it is possible, would seem to be our
obvious priority. While the question of whether and to what extent there is an
innate capacity that could correspond to at least a part of what we mean by
intelligence remains open (and I have not denied that limits may be placed by
nature on an individual's mental capacity - in some cases, at least, they fairly
obviously are), I am presuming, thirdly, that evidence is sufficient to warrant
the conclusion that human intelligence is at least partly a product of circumstance
or environment, including teaching. Even those who define intelligence as an
innate capacity that either is identical to performance on IQ tests or that can only
be assessed by such performance, will have to concede that research in their own
field suggests that IQ scores can be improved. Those who, like me, see strong
reason for rejecting any such view of intelligence, will be even more inclined to
see it as something that can be developed. Fourthly, given that we recognize the
possibility of developing intelligence, I am assuming that such development,
rather than merely classifying students in terms of intelligence, should be the
prime concern of educators. 'To develop the intelligence of students' might even
be the beginning of at least a partial definition of education.

If we start with a dictionary definition of intelligence as the 'capacity for
understanding; ability to perceive and comprehend meaning', it seems
uncontentious to observe that intelligence in this sense is indeed something that
we value, something that we want to develop, something that in some respects at
least we can develop, and something that ought to be of central concern to
educators. The conceptual question is simply this: what in more explicit detail
does this amount to? What conditions have to be met for us to say that someone
has a capacity for understanding that merits the label 'highly intelligent'?
(Perhaps it does not need saying, but we should remember that we are concerned
with the normative sense of intelligence which contrasts it with unintelligent,
rather than the different, neutral, sense of the word that contrasts it with non-

intelligent. It is a feature of being human as contrasted with at least some other species that we have intelligence, so that when faced with a severely brain-damaged individual we may even face the question of whether they are really or fully human.[1] But my concern is less with what distinguishes intelligent from non-intelligent life, than with what is implied by the accolade 'intelligent' or, more explicitly, 'very intelligent'. It may also be noted that intelligence is a degree word. None of us imagines that one either has or does not have high intelligence, or intelligence in the normative sense. We are intelligent to various degrees. None the less, as a way of talking, it is acceptable to think in terms of what distinguishes the intelligent, that is, those of relatively high intelligence, from the unintelligent, that is, those of relatively low intelligence.)

The very first word in this everyday dictionary definition is problematic, as we have already seen *(pp. 30 - 6)*. Reference to 'capacity' or 'ability' is commonplace in our language, and very beguiling. If we are not careful we tend to reify it, assuming that if we refer to a capacity there must be some thing that has some actual existence. Just as the word 'liver' refers to a tangible organ, and the word 'bloodstream' refers to something that can be seen and acted upon, so a capacity for understanding must refer either to some mental organ (or part of the brain) or to some network of physiological interactions, perhaps more obscure and nebulous than, but none the less comparable to, a network of wheels and pulleys.

Obviously, there is something in this way of looking at things (which no doubt partly accounts for our talking this way). It has already been conceded that without the brain the human agent could not be intelligent. Nor would I wish to suggest that questions to do with the functioning of the brain are not of great interest and importance to human scholarship. But it is necessary to raise the question of whether that kind of research and knowledge is of particular importance to those of us whose concern is to articulate an adequate concept of intelligence in the context of education.

If our interest were focused on the education of brain-damaged children, for instance, the matter might be different. But the vast majority of people are alike in having normally functioning brains. Research into normal brain functioning is only going to have direct and immediate repercussions for us to the extent that it reveals limits on what we can hope to achieve or possibilities that we had not envisioned. The claim that different sides of the brain effect different kinds of mental activity, for example, is interesting, but of no real significance to educators who are dealing with students who have both sides functioning normally, and who have no way of interfering with that functioning (and perhaps no right to do so). In the event, this hypothesis has done little more (in educational circles) than give rise to a lot of rather meaningless chatter about some students being primarily right-sided and some left-sided in terms of their brains. But that is simply to use a new vocabulary to say that some are more rational, some more artistic. It does nothing to increase our understanding of what a rational or artistic person is, still less what an intelligent person is, and gives us no clues about how to educate them.

Another problem with a word like 'capacity' is that it is ambiguous as between meaning that 'one can and does do' something and meaning that 'one could, but does not (or does not necessarily)' do something. I have the ability to speak Greek, but what we mean by that is one and the same thing as saying that I do sometimes do it (or have done it). If I had never done it, there could not be grounds for saying that I could. On the other hand, it might be that anybody, by virtue of being human, has the ability or capacity to suffer, even though they never have in fact suffered. It is important to know when reference is made to a capacity for understanding whether what is meant is a potential to acquire understanding (as in the potential to suffer), or rather the fact of understanding (whether it is displayed or not). If the latter is meant, the word 'capacity' becomes more or less redundant and can cease to trouble us. But if the former is meant there are some problems: what does it mean to refer to someone's potential if it has not in fact been realized? How could I know that there is such a potential?

But let us return to the central issue here. If the 'capacity to understand' is supposed to refer to what I have characterized as a physiological set of wheels and pulleys, if, in other words, intelligence is being defined from the outset in terms of some internal process, what are we to say about it? The answer is that we are to reject it, for three reasons.

First, despite the research, which I assume to be entirely beyond reproach in itself, we know very little indeed about this so-called process. When those who are materialistically inclined talk of synapses and neurons as a way of characterizing intelligent behaviour they are offering a description of the functioning of the brain, but they are not explaining why it functions this way nor how it comes to function this way, and still less are they giving us any reason to define intelligence in these terms. A tried and trusted analogy is in order here: when an individual runs fast we say that they are speedy or have speed. 'Having speed' is a way of talking that should not be taken to imply that they actually possess something called speed. They don't. 'To have speed' is to be able to run fast, as evidenced, incidentally, by doing so. The researcher can establish various physical events that occur within the body when the person is running at speed. But we are not thereby tempted to define speed in terms of blood pumping through the heart, muscles contracting, and so on. The researcher is telling us about various physiological occurrences that take place when a person runs fast. He is not telling us anything about what it means to run fast, and no physical entity called speed can be identified. In the same way (and I stress again that I am not denigrating the value of brain research in itself), the suggestion that intelligence is to be defined in terms of a physiological process involves a simple mistake: it is not anything of a material kind; its definition is not to be couched in terms of any kind of material attribute.

The second reason for rejecting such an approach confirms and to some extent justifies the first. The first objection was that it is a mistake to suppose that intelligence needs to be defined in some such way. The second is that, if we think about it, we realize that this is not in fact the kind of thing we mean when we call someone intelligent, nor could it be, since, with the possible exception of the few individuals engaged in brain research, we do not have any idea what is going on in a person's brain when we judge them to be intelligent. When I say that in my view Goethe was a highly intelligent man, it is absolutely clear that I do not mean that he had the 'capacity to understand' in the sense of a highly developed neurophysiological set-up in his body. Fairly clearly, to anticipate, what I primarily mean is that he shows understanding - he understands things.

This brings us to the third reason for objecting to a process view of intelligence. Not only do we know very little about such a process, not only is it evidently not what we typically mean, but also we have other things to worry about that are surely more important in terms of trying to get to grips with the idea of intelligence. What matters, in trying to grasp the concept, is not what goes on in the brain, but what counts as understanding something and what kinds of thing the intelligent person needs to understand. Scientific theory tells us about the atomic structure of a table. But whatever the true scientific account of a table or any other material object, what we *mean* by 'table' is 'a flat, horizontal slab supported by one or more legs', and the conceptual question does not involve us confusing this definition with the scientific theory, but in getting to grips with that definition by asking such things as: can it be any height? What if it has no legs but is suspended from the ceiling? If the slab isn't flat, is it a poor table or not a table at all?

Intelligence, whatever it is, is no more to be defined in terms of the workings of the brain that lie behind it, than the table is to be defined in terms of the atoms that make its existence possible. And the attribution of intelligence no more presupposes an identifiable thing than does the attribution of speed. We attribute intelligence to people who perform certain kinds of mental operation, such as imagining, analysing, synthesizing, recognizing, in certain kinds of way. What we need to be concerned with is what kinds of operation, in relation to what, and in what ways. What kind of imaginative exercise, about what, for example, counts as intelligent?

Recently there has been a resurgence of interest in the possibility of a distinction being drawn between practical and theoretical intelligence, a distinction that goes back to Aristotle.[2] On the face of it, this is a reasonable distinction to make, given that it appears to be a fact of life that some very intelligent academics seem unable to organize their daily lives intelligently, while others, who live intelligently, seem somewhat lacking in any kind of theoretical understanding. However, I would resist making such a distinction for two reasons.

First, despite the superficial plausibility and the undoubted fact that such a distinction could be drawn, certainly in principle and, as we have just seen, probably in fact, none the less the two are very closely related. Practical and theoretical intelligence are intimately related because theory and practice themselves are inextricably interwoven. All practice or action that is other than automatic reaction is theoretical, or has a theoretical backdrop, albeit it may be of a superficial and cursory kind. If I do something for a reason or some set of reasons, that is to say that I am guided by some theoretical considerations. If I turn up to give my lectures on time, that is for some such reason as that I value punctuality, I am afraid of criticism, I want to treat my students well, or I am hoping for promotion, each of which is by definition a theoretical framework. Conversely, good theory is by definition practical: it is supposed to be practicable (though it might not be fashionable, politically acceptable, financially feasible, and suchlike). If my theoretical plan for spanning the gorge leads to a broken bridge and disaster, we do not conclude that this shows how theory and practice are distinct. We say that I am a bad theoretician.

We do not attribute intelligence to people on the strength of a series of actions that are no more than automatic reflexes. A person's life might be conducted intelligently in the sense that the actions performed conform to a pattern such as an intelligent person would choose, but if the person in question performed these actions unwittingly, then while the life can still be accounted intelligent, the agent certainly would not be, because intelligence in any sphere necessarily involves understanding, which implies wittingness. Likewise, the person who refrains from unintelligent choices, such as taking drugs, because they have no opportunity or because they have been indoctrinated against them, does not thereby deserve the label intelligent. To deserve the epithet 'practically intelligent', one must do sensible or appropriate things because one understands them to be so, which is to say in the light of theoretical understanding. To be accounted theoretically intelligent, as has already been intimated, one must theorize intelligently, and theorizing that is impractical or out of touch with reality is not only not intelligent, it isn't even good theory. (A person might of course engage in theoretical work that is so *recherché* as to have little immediate practical utility, but then we should surely be more inclined to describe him as clever or erudite than as intelligent.)

In short, while it cannot be denied that different people show intelligence in different areas of life and that some people, specifically, are more intelligent when it comes to academic study, others when it comes to organizing their daily life, it remains the case that one cannot totally divorce the two: practical intelligence necessarily presupposes some kind of theoretical intelligence, and the latter could hardly be accounted such if it really were quite unrelated to practice. To be sure, we could still make the distinction, although it should now be clear that the difference would be a matter of degree and emphasis rather than a total difference in kind. But it seems inadvisable, given that in practice they shade into one another. There is something unlikely, not to say suspect, about the idea of a lot of people with great practical intelligence but virtually no theoretical intelligence, or vice versa. How can people live their lives with great understanding if they are incapable of theorizing coherently? How could it be that someone with the theoretical intelligence of Einstein could not live his life intelligently if he chose to? (It is not disputed that an Einstein might not be interested in the mundane details of daily life, or that his intelligence might be overcome by laziness or a bad temper. But those are different kinds of point.)

The second reason for rejecting the distinction between practical and theoretical intelligence stems from the fact that intelligence is valued. Broadly speaking we value both so-called theoretical and so-called practical intelligence. Quite apart from the point just made (that they cannot be neatly distinguished) we want people to display both. Indeed, one might go further and suggest that it is itself a mark of intelligence to be concerned about both - to want to cultivate one's mind in theoretical pursuits and to want to conduct one's life intelligently.

Whether that last suggestion is immediately appealing or not, it is surely clear that in any case the question of whether we should distinguish between the theoretical and the practical, and if so which one we should value more, is subsidiary to the larger question of what kinds of understanding we value. Intelligence clearly involves understanding on any account. But understanding of what? Is understanding horse-racing a sign of intelligence? Or understanding atomic physics? Is it the fact that one can understand what one chooses to understand that matters, or does the intelligent person by definition have to understand certain kinds of thing rather than others? In broad terms, the answer that I shall provide suggests that intelligent people are those who have understanding of matters that are, in various degrees, complex, intrinsically valued, and of practical utility - matters moreover that speak to the nature of the world and the human condition. Intelligence is very much to be defined in terms of what we understand rather than the mere fact that we can display understanding.

Intelligence, Speed, and Problem Solving

Before pursuing that line of thought there are some other suggestions to be considered. Speed has already been referred to briefly *(see pp. 28 - 9)*, and notwithstanding Jensen's claim that there is no contingent link worthy of note between people's ability to perform well on standardized tests of achievement and their ability to move their fingers rapidly, many people do want to argue that speed of intellectual response should be part of the definition of intelligence. The quick repartee, the swift uptake, the rapid digestion of information, the speedy calculation, and suchlike are seen by many as part of what is meant by calling someone intelligent. If we see reason to define intelligence partly by reference to this criterion, empirical research becomes irrelevant to the question of whether reaction time (of a certain sort) is related: it is so by definition, in which case a test of people's reaction time would serve the quite different function of being one way to determine that some people lack intelligence. It could not establish that anyone was intelligent, since there is more to intelligence than speed of reaction, on any view; but it could establish that certain people were not intelligent. (We should add that the particular test devised by Jensen would not be relevant, since the kind of speed of reaction we are here considering is quite different from that which he tested. There seems no obvious reason to suggest that rapid physical response to a visual stimulus is part of what we mean by intelligence, and we have no independent evidence that that kind of speed of reaction is in any way related to the kinds of speedy intellectual response that concern us.)

But is speed of mental operation part of the characterization of intelligence? Are we persuaded by the quite common view that it should be? *Prima facie*, it does seem to be a relevant consideration - there is an oddity, at any rate at first blush, about the idea that we would account an individual who was notably slow in the uptake, ponderous in response, and the like, as intelligent. But we need to bear in mind the distinction between defining characteristics and symptoms of a concept. A sore throat may be a symptom of a number of different ailments, and in some cases it is not even a necessary symptom. Thus, if the patient has a sore throat it may suggest to us that they are suffering from flu or mumps, and it may be that they *are* suffering from one or the other. But equally they might not be. A sore throat is not a defining characteristic of either, since it is neither a necessary nor a sufficient condition of either. Perhaps, in the same way, speed of reaction should be seen as a useful indicator of intelligence without being part of the meaning of the term. Perhaps, that is to say, it often coincides with intelligence, but not necessarily so.

If Shakespeare were to be alive today and he turned out to be dull and slow as an after-dinner companion, we surely would not on those grounds revise our estimate of him as a highly intelligent individual. That judgement is based on the evidence of his plays which show him to have been a person of insight, with considerable understanding of the human condition, a strong grasp of diverse important matters, and a considerable artistic talent, all of which seem to count for rather more, in this context, than the question of how easily or rapidly he worked, or more generally his quickness of uptake. Indeed, if such speed were crucial to the meaning of intelligent, we would not be in a position to make judgements about the intelligence of Shakespeare or any other individual with whom we were not personally acquainted. Yet we have no hesitation in making judgements about a whole variety of historical and contemporary figures whom we know only through their work and, consequently, whose speed of thought is unknown to us. Conversely, knowing someone to have a quick wit is insufficient grounds for judging them to be intelligent, since it is possible to be a master of the repartee, and yet lack any deep understanding, broad sympathy, insight, common sense, or grasp of reality, some at least of which would seem, by contrast, to be closely tied up with what we mean by 'intelligence'.

It therefore seems more plausible to say that certain kinds of speed in mental activity are contingently related to intelligence, treating such speed as a possible indication of intelligence, and lack of it as a possible sign of unintelligence, but that it is not actually part of the meaning of the term. As so often, an element of degree comes into this. The person who struggles for hours to devise a humorous anecdote may indeed thereby indicate that he is less intelligent than the more natural raconteur; the individual who takes a lifetime to acquire a basic understanding of physics may thereby indicate that they are less intelligent than the person who acquires some such understanding over a period of three years' study. But still we do not have to define intelligence in terms of such speed.[3]

The temptation to see speed as part of the meaning of intelligence is part of the wider temptation to define this and other mental concepts in terms of a process *(see pp. 42 - 8)*. Of course, in a sense, process *is* involved: if one is intelligent or creative or imaginative one proceeds intelligently, creatively, or imaginatively. The objection to trying to define the concepts in terms of process is that we know very little about such processes and in fact largely infer them from achievements, from which they cannot in any case be divorced. Our judgement that Leonardo da Vinci was highly creative is not, and could not be, based upon knowledge of how his mind worked. It is based on knowledge of what he produced. To say that he was highly creative is to say that he produced highly creative works of various sorts. Granted that they came about as a result of a mental process on his part, that is not what we are referring to when we call him creative. The process, whatever it was, that led to the painting of the *Mona Lisa* is only valuable because it led to such a product; it cannot be considered in isolation from some such achievement (how could one go through the creative process without doing anything or producing anything creative? What on earth would it mean?); and in any case we know nothing about Leonardo's mental process, but that does not stop us recognizing his creativity.

The suggestion here, then, is that it is truer to the way we actually operate (notwithstanding the unreflective and widespread use of process language amongst educators) to define intelligence in terms of what people have come to understand, rather than in terms of the speed with which they acquire understanding or the speed with which they utilize or display it on particular occasions. An intelligent historian has a good historical understanding, which in turn allows him to pursue historical study intelligently. Because he has that understanding at his fingertips, so to speak, he will in all likelihood proceed relatively quickly and efficiently in his research; but if he did not, if he happened to be very painstaking, methodical, and ultimately slow, we surely wouldn't be inclined to reverse our estimate of his intelligence.

Not only does it seem on reflection to be inappropriate to include speed of mental operations in the definition of intelligence, there is also a practical advantage in not doing so (and we should remember that analysing a concept is a matter of making decisions by criteria that include utility). We must avoid the tendency to put all our eggs in one basket, which in this context means all our values in one concept. To be sure, we value swift repartee and the like, but why make it part of the meaning of intelligence? We have other concepts such as cleverness, brightness, and wit, which serve to pinpoint related but distinct mental activity. If intelligence is defined in such a way as to include all the mental virtues, it becomes too general a term to serve any particular purpose.

A closely related issue, since it has something to do with the problem of defining mental faculties in terms of process, is that of generic skills. We have already referred to the tendency, particularly amongst psychologists, to define intelligence in terms of certain abstract generalized skills such as problem solving, recognizing relationships, synthesizing, and the like. As a casual and superficial way of talking there is nothing wrong with this tendency. People solve problems; why should we not refer to their problem-solving ability or skill? No reason at all, if that is all we are doing. The danger comes if we assume that such a mental skill is comparable in all respects to a physical skill, if we reify the ability and assume that there is some tangible part of the brain that simply does the problem solving in an automatic way, if we assume that it can be divorced from a particular context, and if, consequently, we assume that in so far as a person has the ability they have it and can use it in all situations. If we make any of these assumptions we are building up an unwarranted and false picture of the way in which the human mind actually works, and we will inevitably be drawn to conducting inappropriate kinds of research, making inappropriate judgements, and suggesting inappropriate ways of teaching and developing the mind.

A physical skill, such as juggling, waggling one's ears, dribbling a soccer ball, or sleight of hand, is an ability that is self-contained and can be rehearsed, practised, and developed in itself, and subsequently put to use more or less whenever and wherever one chooses. It is also relatively unconnected to understanding: one does not have to understand much about the theory behind juggling to become very skilful at it. In all these respects a so-called mental skill is quite different. It is not self-contained and perfectible in itself: one cannot practise solving problems, as one can practise waggling one's ears; one has to practise solving particular problems, because the idea of problem solving without a problem doesn't make sense. Problem solving and all other mental concepts are also very closely tied up with understanding: to solve a problem it is necessary to understand it. Consequently one may practise and perfect solving a certain kind of problem, say mathematical, and be no nearer being able to solve a different kind of problem such as a moral problem.

It follows from the previous point that even if the capacity to solve problems can be associated with some particular part of the brain, so that, put simply, if that part of the brain is damaged the individual is incapable of solving any problem, none the less solving problems is not simply a matter of the brain functioning in a certain way, as juggling might be said to be essentially a matter of the body functioning in a certain kind of way. The human mind is not a machine that, already programmed like the computer, spews out the answer to a problem automatically. Because solving problems necessarily involves understanding, we cannot meaningfully locate the problem-solving ability in physical or physiological terms. It is not a mental organ, akin to a physical organ such as the heart that simply gets on with the job of pumping blood in an automatic fashion; and, because the ability to solve problems involves understanding, it cannot be divorced from particular contexts, which means in turn that one cannot be said simply to have the ability, with the implied corollary that one can put it to use whenever and wherever one wishes. One can only have the ability to solve particular kinds of problem, and the fact that one has that ability tells us nothing about the likelihood of one's having the ability to solve quite different kinds of problem.

It is true that some individuals can solve all manner of problems, and we may therefore refer to them as being good problem solvers in general. But such people still do not have some general capacity; it is merely a contingent fact that they have wide understanding and are therefore able to solve all manner of problems. It is true also that some very general characteristics may be said to be common to all instances of problem solving, such as, perhaps, the ability to consider evidence, willingness to apply oneself, or, one might say, the capacity to think. But such qualities as may be thought to be common to all instances are each insufficient in themselves to characterize the concept of problem solving, and in any case, to be operative, they require understanding. I may have the disposition to consider evidence, but I cannot do so if I do not understand the nature of the evidence.

Empirically, notwithstanding the example of a polymath such as Leonardo da Vinci, we know that people are not necessarily good at problem solving (or bad at it) without qualification. They are good (or bad) at solving certain kinds of problem. But the point being made is that, although so much is a matter of common observation, it is not just a contingent fact about the world that might have been different. It is a matter of logical necessity. You cannot solve a problem, whatever the state of your brain, if you lack relevant understanding, and understanding can be of quite different kinds and is certainly something that has to be acquired. Nor is it just a question of applying the general ability in different contexts. Even possession of a physical skill such as a sense of balance does not guarantee that one can perform any activity that requires balance, from ballet to steeplejacking. Balance is not a uniform quality that is utilized 'as is' in both trapeze work and ballet; it takes a different form in each case and some who are generally thought to have a sense of balance will none the less have to learn to utilize it in ballet (and may conceivably fail to do so). Even more obviously with mental abilities, it is not a question of simply having to acquire new information on which to set one's problem-solving skills to work. It is not parallel to having a spade with which you can dig in sand, earth, or clay as the mood strikes you. It is a question of understanding the different nature of different kinds of problem and coming to grips with the distinctively appropriate manner of solving them.

The conclusion to be drawn from these observations is that while it may be the case that the ability to solve problems (think critically, be creative, and so on) can be related to particular parts of the brain, while some people may have brains so constituted that they are in principle more capable than others of becoming good problem solvers, while there are certain general features common to all instances of problem solving, and while some people undoubtedly do show a talent for solving problems, in a wide variety of contexts, - while all such claims may be valid, to focus on them is perverse in the extreme, when it is

certain that none of these factors can be examined except when they are operating in specific contexts, and that they cannot operate in a context where understanding is lacking. It follows that if our concern is with developing such capacities we have to concentrate on developing understanding. The serious practical question that then arises is whether in that case it is sensible to make use of the tests and exercises relating to problem solving, critical thinking, and creativity that are typically to be found, given that they are deliberately designed to concentrate on problems that are relatively simple, non-specialized, and detached, rather than on complex problems that presuppose sophisticated understanding. Is it wiser to encourage students to engage in problem-solving exercises that are designed for no other purpose than to give them the opportunity to solve problems, and that do not presuppose any particular kind of complex understanding or study, or to encourage them to develop the understanding necessary to get to grips with real problems in morality, war, marriage, friendship, death, history, science, and the like?

Notes and references

1. Kieran Egan queries whether it isn't obvious that the offspring of humans are humans. But this is to confuse the normative and non-normative senses of 'human'. It also ignores the point considered above, that circumstances might require that we make a decision in respect of the classification of some unexpected attributes of the offspring.
2. This interest is shown both in the psychological literature, e.g., Sternberg, R.J., (1985), *Beyond I.Q.: a triarchic theory of human intelligence*, Cambridge: Cambridge University Press, and in the educational literature, e.g., Hirst, P.H., 'Education, Knowledge and Practices', in Barrow, R. and White, P. (eds), (1993), *Beyond Liberal Education*, London: Routledge.
3. I am not as certain of this claim as the exigencies of writing a book that presents a tolerably clear set of ideas have led me to suggest. I recognize, for example, that many would be inclined to distinguish between the intelligence of two students precisely by reference to the relative speed with which either one seems to grasp an idea. None the less, I incline to the view that, while widely associated with intelligence, speed should not be seen as a defining characteristic.

4. The Concept of Intelligence

Intelligence and Understanding

In the light of what has been said about the notion of there being generic mental skills, the idea of conceptualizing the intellect in terms of process, and the particular question of whether speed of mental response should be considered a defining characteristic of intelligence, I would now suggest that it is indeed clear, as was suggested when the issue of practical and theoretical intelligence was raised, that the crucial conceptual question is: what understanding? Intelligence is to be defined in terms of what one understands, but is it a question of how much one understands or of what kinds of thing one understands?

If nothing is to be said about types of understanding, the concept is so broad as to be of little practical value, since everybody, in having some understanding, would have a degree of intelligence, and nobody would come anywhere near the ideal, since nobody understands all that there is to be understood.[1] Any attempt to distinguish between people's intelligence in terms of quantity alone would prove impossible in practice: how does one begin to assess how much understanding a person has, if we have to take into account their rational understanding of various kinds of argument and theory, their understanding of people, their understanding of nature, their understanding of themselves, their understanding of art, and so on? How, indeed, would one set about making a quantitative assessment of their knowledge even in one of these areas, such as understanding of art? Not only is it doubtful whether any such assessment could be made in a coherent way, it is not in fact by reference to such an assessment that we do attempt to make judgements about people's intelligence. The process view of intelligence is right to this extent at least: our judgements relate more to how people use their minds than to an estimate of how much they know. Besides, since intelligence is a normative term, and since, by definition, we do not see any particular merit in a mass of trivial and worthless understanding, it is clear that there is an issue of quality. The mere fact that someone knows how to service an automobile, has rapport with animals, and can speak a foreign language, is no reason to conclude that they are necessarily intelligent. Neither the individual who has a massive understanding of physics nor the individual who has all the information contained in the *Guinness Book of Records* is necessarily intelligent.

If the concept is going to be useful to us and if it is going to merit its normative overtones, it will be necessary to characterize the understanding it involves in a way that is manageable and in harmony with our values, and in a way that explains how we can make reasonable judgements about people's intelligence, without needing a full inventory of the knowledge they possess.

The first thing we need to do is to distinguish between the different sorts of understanding involved in understanding arguments, understanding people, understanding art, and so forth. All of these different types of understanding may very well be valuable, and some might argue that, say, understanding people (meaning something like having an intuitive sympathy with people, being able to appreciate the way they are, and to get on with them) is more important than rational understanding of argument. But whatever relative value we may attach to various different types of understanding in this sense, intelligence is surely essentially and primarily to be defined in terms of rational understanding. The fact that somebody has great artistic understanding in the sense of appreciation of art does not in itself lead us to conclude that they are intelligent, and conversely one can imagine someone being highly intelligent who happened not to have any feeling for art at all. Similarly, even if one were to value the ability to get on with people rather more than the ability to follow arguments, reason well, and so forth, one could none the less concede that intelligence has more to do with the latter than the former. When we pick out historical examples of intelligent people, Socrates seems more appropriate than St Francis, even if we happen to admire the latter more.

The distinctions made in the previous paragraph are no doubt somewhat artificial. It is, for example, very likely the case that getting on with people is enhanced by a reasonable degree of rational understanding. One might even argue that it is necessarily involved, and similarly in the case of appreciating art. None the less, one can differentiate between what I have called rational understanding and understanding of people, art, nature, or religion in the sense of 'having a feeling for', and it seems clear that the former is crucial to what we mean by intelligence in a way that the latter are not.[2]

But still the realm of rational understanding is far too large and diffuse to allow us to make meaningful judgements about people's intelligence without further refinement. Everybody has rational understanding of many things. How are we to distinguish between two people's intelligence by reference to their stock of rational understanding? (It is clear that we are not really concerned with their stock of information. People are not necessarily particularly intelligent because they know a lot in this sense, and, conversely, a person who happens to have a very small stock of facts, figures, and such-like information might be judged to be intelligent.)

It may help at this point to consider what would lead us to call somebody relatively unintelligent. Unintelligent people are not to be confused with ignorant people. Unintelligent people are so-called largely because they display a capacity to misunderstand, in the sense of get their thinking wrong. They fail to grasp arguments, to proceed logically, to take account of evidence that is brought to their attention, to recognize evidence as evidence. In particular, they deal with problems or issues in inappropriate kinds of way, as when a person insists that a painting is a work of high quality because it sells for a large sum of money, failing to see that economic considerations or considerations of popularity are irrelevant to the issue of the quality of a work of art.

The intelligent person is one who is able to engage in rational argument in a way that observes the rules of sound reasoning. (We are not, incidentally, suggesting that the intelligent person is necessarily rational all the time. Intelligent people can quite as easily grow bored, lose their tempers, curb their tongue out of politeness, as anyone else. An intelligent person is one who is capable of engaging in sound reasoning should he choose to do so.)

The question therefore becomes whether there is a way of characterizing the important elements in the ability to reason soundly about matters of importance that would make it possible for us to make reasonable judgements about people's intelligence in the sort of way that we do.

This question cannot be satisfactorily answered in terms of a list of important topics or issues. Any such list would be unmanageably large, highly contentious, and would represent an ideal to which few if any could aspire. More to the point, such a list would not be in accord with the way in which we in fact ascribe intelligence. Environmental and gender issues, for example, would probably be widely regarded as important topics today. But it is neither necessary nor sufficient to being intelligent that one should be informed about and competent at debating these particular issues. It is not necessary, because surely an individual who for some reason or another happened never to have come across environmental debate might none the less be intelligent. It is not sufficient because a person might be very well informed, erudite, and sensible on such issues, but still strike us on balance as rather unintelligent. One can well imagine saying, 'It's funny. Old so and so is very sound on these two particular topics, and yet he is otherwise such a complete idiot'. The reason that we would be reluctant to call people intelligent on the grounds of their good sense on these two topics alone is that intelligence is a general term and a term of the highest praise. (A general term, which means a broad one, is not to be confused with a generic term.) 'Intelligent' is, if nothing else, our word for describing people

whom we consider to have understanding of important matters across a broad spectrum. It is, in other words, part of the meaning of the word that people who are intelligent should have broad understanding and understanding of whatever can be shown to be of fundamental importance. Intelligence lies less in being well versed in argument on certain topical issues than in having the kind of understanding that allows one to engage successfully (intelligently) with all manner of topics as they come and go, and as their importance waxes and wanes.

Nor should we make the mistake of equating intelligence with various particular talents and competencies. Brilliance at science, great success in politics, creative artistic talent, highly competent management, and so forth may all be praiseworthy, but they do not necessarily betoken intelligence.

If we are to distinguish intelligence from being well informed, being sensible, being clever, being wise, being sound on particular issues (and it is part of the point of analysis to distinguish between related but distinct ideas), then we need to depict the necessary understanding in terms of certain basic types or necessary modes of rational understanding that transcend particular issues. If people do display intelligence in relation to environmental issues, for example, that will be because they show philosophical acumen, historical awareness, a scientific grasp, and so forth. Because of the nature of these types of understanding, if a person can display them in the context of environmental issues then one would expect him to be able to utilize them in relation to other issues, if he chose to do so. If this is not in fact the case, then one must assume that the apparent understanding in this case was not true understanding, but rather the regurgitation of intelligent responses (i.e., responses that an intelligent person would make) acquired by some means such as indoctrination or rote-learning, in which case the individual is not truly intelligent. (For we must repeat that it is possible to do intelligent things without being intelligent, notwithstanding the fact that we ascribe intelligence to people on the strength of how they perform.)

The position we are moving towards is that an intelligent person is one who has broad understanding of certain fundamental ways of thinking that structure our way of looking at the world. It is, incidentally, an unashamed declaration that there is a crucial conceptual link between intelligence and a liberal education. But before giving a more detailed account of what these ways of understanding may be, I need to comment briefly on the claim that such things as philosophical acumen or historical awareness can be utilized in a variety of contexts across the board.

It may seem that this is to make the very mistake that I criticized when arguing against the idea of generic mental skills *(see pp. 50 - 3)*. Am I not in fact introducing the generic skill of philosophizing in place of that of problem solving and the like? The answer is no, and the difference is this: the idea of a generic skill of problem solving is misconceived because problems are of different logical kinds (they need solving in radically different kinds of way). The ways of thinking that I am about to introduce represent the different logical kinds of problem in question. Some problems are scientific, others are philosophical (and some of course are complex and involve scientific, philosophical, and other elements). If one has philosophical ability then one is able to deal with most philosophical problems, or philosophical aspects of problems, wherever one meets them, because to a large extent philosophizing is an abstract activity that does not depend upon particular knowledge. Thus, as a philosopher, I know the kinds of moves I have to make in analysing a concept whether the concept be love, education, or justice. Similarly, if I have scientific understanding (of a general kind to do with the scientific mode of inquiry), then whether the problem we face is about the environment or gender issues, I am in a position to proceed scientifically where appropriate. If I have historical awareness and competence, then whatever the historical question may be about, I know how to proceed. I may require new information, but I do not need to acquire understanding of a new kind of inquiry.

It is true that a philosopher who knew no science would be seriously impaired in trying to philosophize about science. But the claim here is that there is a determinate (and in fact rather small) number of ways of understanding that between them encompass all that we are capable of understanding. Thus, it is philosophical acumen in conjunction with certain other types of understanding, such as the historical and the scientific, that gives an individual the ability to cope with any kind of problem. This is quite different from maintaining that there is some mysterious processing ability (or set of skills) that enables one to cope with any kind of problem. In fact it is not only different, it is, so to speak, the reason why the idea of a generic problem-solving skill doesn't make sense. It is because there are philosophical questions, scientific questions, and historical questions, which do not merely have different subject matter but which operate in quite different ways, that it does not make sense to talk of a general capacity to answer questions or solve problems.

There are certain developed traditions of inquiry that structure our understanding. It could well have been different, it could change tomorrow, but, as things stand, human beings see the world in terms of only a limited number of kinds of question and ways of dealing with them. To be precise: we recognize scientific questions and we regard a certain kind of procedure as appropriate to dealing with a scientific question. We recognize philosophical questions, and we believe that these have to be examined in a way that is quite different from scientific questions. We recognize mathematical questions, and

that they have to be dealt with on their own terms. We recognize historical questions, and that they are not answered by simple application of the techniques of the scientist, or the philosopher, or the mathematician. We recognize aesthetic questions, which, again seem to be *sui generis*, we recognize moral questions, and we recognize religious or metaphysical questions, and, even if we happen to believe that religion is bunk, we realize that operating within that sphere is logically quite different from doing science, history, etc. And, finally, we recognize that literature deals with questions about the human condition that can only be addressed in this distinctive way that blends the conjectural and the proven, the intuitive and the demonstrated, the particular and the general, description and interpretation. One can pursue scientific investigations into love, friendship, or envy, one can consider them historically, one can analyse them in the manner of the philosopher, but still there remains the possibility of trying to understand them in a different way through the creative attempt to depict them in detailed imaginative case studies.

The eight distinguishable traditions of inquiry that I introduce here might well be classified in slightly different ways, and there are a number of interesting and important questions about this classification that might reasonably be raised. One obvious question is what precisely is meant by, say, the 'philosophical', and can it in practice be neatly divorced from, say, the 'literary'? Or again, will it really do to set a fairly well-established discipline such as mathematics, which seems unique to almost everybody, alongside a so-called literary discipline, when to many people literature and the study of literature are pretty hazy notions?

Good questions, indeed. But not germane to the present issue. The importance of this thesis is that it is true as far as it goes (which does not mean that there are not other equally valid ways of describing our understanding, only that this is one way that has validity), and that it enables us to conceptualize intelligence, devise school curricula, and so forth, in meaningful and practical ways.

What the thesis essentially maintains is that of all the questions one might ask about anything, we cannot currently conceive of one that would not have to be examined by a scientific, historical, aesthetic, moral, literary, metaphysical, mathematical, or philosophical type of inquiry (or some amalgam of these), in that we do not know of any other rational mode of inquiry. Someone might say, but there are political questions, and of course there are political questions, just as there are gardening questions, feminist questions, existentialist questions, phenomenological questions, sociological questions, sports questions, economic questions, and so on. But these are political questions in the sense of questions about politics. They are not questions that have to be dealt with in a clearly distinguishable manner, because political questions (gardening, feminist, sociological questions, etc.) will all turn out to be questions that have to be approached scientifically, philosophically, mathematically, etc., or to be complex problems that need to be broken down and their constituent parts dealt with scientifically, philosophically, etc.

Traditions of Rational Inquiry and Understanding

Because of the importance of this thesis in my overall argument, and because it is a thesis of a type that is still hotly disputed by some, I shall now approach it once again from a slightly different angle and in slightly more detail.

One of the most fundamental distinctions in our thinking is that between the empirical and the conceptual. Some claims that we make about the world are based upon, and need to be assessed by, the use of the senses, particularly observation. We explore such claims through experiment. Claims that fall into this category may range from abstruse hypotheses in the natural sciences to everyday commonsense claims such as that one's spouse is in the garden-shed. There is an enormous variety of techniques of experiment, a thousand different kinds of empirical inquiry that might be engaged in. None the less all claims of this type are radically different from conceptual claims, such as the question of whether intelligence is to be defined in terms of understanding, the main feature of which is that the evidence of the senses is ultimately irrelevant. To deal with the latter kind of question one does not need to involve oneself in any kind of observation or experiment. To do so would be quite inappropriate and betray a major misunderstanding. Not only is this distinction fundamental, it is also commonly not appreciated, and, consequently, the direct cause of major mistakes in reasoning. We have already seen that failure to understand and recognize the distinction has been the cause of considerable confusion and misleading pronouncements in respect of intelligence *(see Chapter 2)*, but the failure of people to argue coherently about all manner of topics because they neither understand the distinction nor see the importance of conceptual argument, or know how to carry it out, is an everyday occurrence. Almost any topical debate about people's rights, abortion, the environment, and so on, will reveal evidence of a widespread inability to recognize, appreciate, and handle the conceptual dimension. We may, therefore, say that one dimension of the understanding that characterizes intelligence would be the ability to distinguish the empirical from the conceptual, to recognize either one when it crops up, and to be able to deal with each in the appropriate manner. To put it in terms of a simple example, intelligent people can recognize that the claim that 'there is human life on the moon' is different in kind, and not just subject matter, from the claim that 'intelligence involves understanding', and know the appropriate way to deal with either one in principle, even if, as may often be the case, and for a variety of reasons, they are not actually able to explore and examine either one in practice.

It might be argued that all other developed disciplines or systems of thought are sub-species of either the empirical or the conceptual, or involve both.[3] In other words, one might argue that subjects such as mathematics, politics, history, Marxism, environmental studies, sociology, psychology, art, and phenomenology are all defined in terms of their distinctive subject matter combined with an empirical mode of inquiry, a conceptual one, or a combination of both. If that were all there was to be said, this particular inquiry into the kind of understanding that characterizes intelligence would come to a rapid halt, because if that is all there is to be said, we would be left with a conception of intelligence that would still be of little practical value. To suggest that intelligent people should be adept at recognizing and dealing with all empirical claims, all conceptual claims, and all hybrids (i.e., every other kind of claim), would be to ask too much. On the other hand, if all those who can deal with the empirical and conceptual in some subject matter or other, be it politics, stamp-collecting, art, cookery, or mathematics, are to be accounted intelligent, then the word will not serve to discriminate: almost everybody will be intelligent. Even if we had a way of quantifying people's ability in these various subjects, which we don't, we should simply be saying that to be intelligent means to be good at some subject, never mind what. But that is not what we mean by intelligence. It is not equivalent to specialist understanding of one sort or another. On the contrary, part of our conception of intelligence is that intelligent people can deal with all manner of problems, questions, or claims in an adequate way. We therefore need to consider whether there is a way of giving further specification to the kind of understanding that characterizes intelligence, such that intelligent people can be said to understand some things rather than others. Can we provide reasons, for example, for concluding that an intelligent person needs to have a grasp of mathematics, but not necessarily of sociology?

The answer is that we can, by making use of the two criteria of theoretical depth and theoretical extent. What I mean by these terms can be illustrated by reference to a model of empirical inquiry such as the natural sciences and a model of conceptual inquiry such as philosophy. The natural sciences, taken as a whole (and ignoring the fact that some aspects such as theoretical physics are in fact conceptual rather than empirical), are centred on the use of empirical means to increase our understanding of natural phenomena. The discipline has theoretical depth in that scientific theory, having been developed, argued over, and minutely considered for centuries, now represents a highly sophisticated and powerful body of theory. It is true that now, as at any other period of history, there are important disagreements about the nature of such theory, and there is no reason to suppose that our understanding of it will not alter in future years. None the less, there is a common understanding of scientific theory and it is not something that an individual comes by easily. To understand scientific theory involves coming to grips with a sophisticated network of complex and subtle concepts and ideas. In that sense it is theoretically deep in a way that, say, the theory of cooking is not. It is also, despite the ongoing debate, more coherent and compact than, say, literary theory at the present time. Literary theory does not present a hard core of agreement, with challenging debates on the perimeter, as science does, so much as a whole host of widely different views of the nature of literature, the point of studying it, and approaches to studying it. It is theoretically diverse rather than theoretically deep. Philosophy, on the other hand, though it has its rival schools and competing techniques, is, like science, if only for historical reasons, a subject that has a rich, developed, and complex core that gives it theoretical depth.[4]

Science and philosophy also deal in issues that have wide relevance and that cover much of our understanding. That is to say the subject matter of either one covers a large part of what we want to know and their findings have wide-ranging relevance. That is essentially what is meant by theoretical extent. To know all that there is to know about the genre of mystery stories or popular music, by contrast, is to know about a very small corner of our world and it is knowledge that does not have much utility in respect of other aspects of our lives. Such subjects are lacking in theoretical extent.

Now clearly, if we could agree upon a manageable number of subjects or disciplines that were rich in theoretical depth and extent, we could reasonably characterize the understanding that is essential to intelligence in terms of those subjects, because we would have isolated certain types of understanding that have a wide significance and that are not lightly come by. That is appropriate since intelligence is not lightly come by and has a wide significance.

Working with these criteria we can rapidly see that mathematics has both. To be unable to cope with number, quantity, shape, and space is fairly obviously to be unable to proceed intelligently in a wide variety of situations (theoretical extent). But mathematics is not something that, generally speaking, individuals come to grips with easily. It is in fact one of the most highly developed of disciplines, involving a notation system and a complex network of sophisticated concepts such that one may naturally be inclined to regard mastery of the field as a greater intellectual achievement than mastery of, say, horticulture. Mathematics, in short, is distinct from empirical and conceptual inquiry, involves a number of *sui generis* claims, is of wide significance, and has to be understood on its own terms. One does not come to understand the meaning of claims such as that the area of a circle = IIr^2 by looking at a lot of circles or raising the philosopher's question 'what is a circle?'. One does it by coming to grips with mathematics.

Aesthetics, similarly, represents a subject that has theoretical depth and extent. We are not talking here directly about aesthetic appreciation, but about aesthetic understanding. However, the two are closely related. While it may be debated whether and to what extent the latter is necessary to the former, it is certainly the case that aesthetic understanding can lead to and enhance aesthetic appreciation. But to understand aesthetics is not the matter of a moment. There is a developed and complex body of theory that one has to come to grips with. Having done so, one is in a position to understand a dimension of life that has relevance over a wide area.

There is, it is true, a certain similarity between an aesthetic claim and a conceptual claim, since a claim such as that 'the *Mona Lisa* is beautiful' depends upon meaning as well as upon observation. The art critic, the connoisseur, and the private individual need to clarify what they mean by 'beautiful', in addition to comparing the *Mona Lisa* with other paintings, or devising some other kind of empirical test. But there are at least two crucial differences: first, ultimately the claim does depend upon the painting, and anyone interested in considering its plausibility would need to learn to look at the painting; secondly, the question of what constitutes beauty, the conceptual question, must be approached in the light of a well-established tradition. We can reject the views of the past, but a claim such as that the *Mona Lisa* is beautiful gains part of its meaning from the context of the historical development of the tradition of aesthetics. Putting it crudely, whereas anyone with philosophical competence can address the question of whether it is reasonable to claim that to be intelligent is to have breadth of understanding, only those who also have a grasp of the *sui generis* tradition of aesthetic discourse and art are in a position to assess this claim meaningfully. Anyone can have a view, and any philosopher could offer an abstract analysis of the concept of beauty, but the claim is made in the context of a particular tradition of understanding, and can only be given serious consideration by those who know that context.

The logic of religious and moral claims is more or less identical. The claim that 'the Pope is infallible', for example, is certainly philosophical rather than scientific. There is nothing we can do with the Pope in the laboratory to see if it is true, since we all know that whatever the claim means, it is not apparently invalidated by the transparent fact that, in common parlance, Popes are forever making mistakes. Once again, the point is that we are not in the realm of common parlance, but in the realm of a highly specialized and developed language that needs to be understood on its own terms, because it works in its own way. Religion, in all its manifestations, has given rise to a language in which claims are made that clearly cannot be assessed by those who do not take the trouble to understand the network of concepts lying at the heart of such a way of looking at the world. Exactly the same has to be said about moral claims. Whether it is true, false, descriptive, emotive, or mere gibberish, the claim that 'rape is morally evil' is not determined by observation or experiment, is not resolved by mathematical moves, is not an aesthetic question, is not a religious question, and yet cannot be settled by the mere exercise of philosophical analysis. It is a claim that belongs within, and cannot be divorced from, a rich and extensive network of concepts and beliefs, and that network, the product of centuries of thought of a distinctive kind, is the tradition of moral understanding that one has to come to grips with in order to make an intelligible response to such a claim.

A historical claim, such as that 'the Tsar's conduct caused the Russian Revolution' is to some degree a contingent one, to be determined in principle by experiment and observation rather than by philosophy.[5] But many claims about the past fairly obviously cannot be easily, if at all, tested in the sorts of way that we can test current empirical claims. Here the issue is not so much mastering a language, but mastering an understanding of similar situations and claims. To assess a historical claim one has to be versed in history, obviously in the sense that one needs to know about the relevant period in the past, but also in that one needs to understand the business of history. This makes history a distinctive mode of inquiry in a way that is slightly different from the way in which the others so far considered are distinctive modes of inquiry. But the claim is not that each of these types of inquiry is distinctive by exactly the same criteria or in exactly the same way. The claim is only that they are, in their different ways, distinct and fundamental to our way of understanding the world. One cannot assess a historical claim if one is ignorant of history; by contrast, though it might be disadvantageous, it is possible to assess a political claim, a sociological claim, or a psychological claim, without being a student of politics, sociology, or psychology, provided that one is furnished with the immediately relevant data and has a sound grasp of the fundamental modes of inquiry referred to here. For example, although not a sociologist and perhaps lacking some of the relevant research data pertaining to the claim that 'social background is the key determinant of school success', a person might fully understand the nature of the claim and the way in which it would need to be examined (as well, in this case, as the fact that it is not a claim that can be conclusively verified or falsified). Similarly, while a person's lack of political interest, experience, and wisdom might make his immediate views on proportional representation, nationalism, or free trade less than compelling, his ability to talk intelligently about such things is governed by his conceptual ability, his historical understanding, his understanding of the empirical, and so on, rather than by his study of politics *per se*.

Historians will dispute the nature of history, perhaps more than most practitioners of other disciplines dispute the nature of theirs. Perhaps it should be seen simply as the application of particular kinds of empirical technique to the past, perhaps as a unique form of conceptual inquiry, perhaps as a combination of both. Perhaps it should be seen as *sui generis*. But, however it is seen, historical understanding clearly has theoretical depth and extent to a high degree, in as much as it requires prolonged and careful study and can illuminate a vast number of problems and issues. There is always a historical dimension to a problem, and in many cases it is of considerable importance.

The claim that 'love and friendship are incompatible' is not necessarily a distinctive kind of claim (it could be treated as empirical or philosophical, for example), but it furnishes an example of a claim that might need to be assessed in a way that is distinct from any of the seven so far mentioned - namely by means of imaginative literature. Some of the most important claims that human beings want to consider - claims very often about human relations, or, more generally, the human condition - cannot be examined as matters for straightforward observation, cannot be analysed in the abstract, cannot be interpreted as moral or religious claims, and so on, but are claims that can only really be studied, examined, and considered by the attempt to project an imaginative and detailed case study for the reader's reflective, but intuitive, reaction. Some things can only be thought about. Literature is the name we give to that *corpus* of thought that has been devoted to such matters.[6]

Literature, regardless of one's views about current academic disputes concerning literary theory, represents an enormous body of knowledge, related in particular to the overarching question of what it is to be human, and a host of derivative questions about personal relationships, self-identity, expression, communication, and the like. Other kinds of question can of course be asked about all these topics. One can research the history of friendship, for example; one can analyse the concept of friendship, and one can conduct empirical investigations into friendship. But literature offers something unique: the imaginative exploration and depiction of case studies in friendship. Naturally, the value of literature's contribution to increasing our understanding of friendship or anything else is dependent on the quality of the author's understanding as well as his skill in communicating it. But, regardless of inevitable disagreements about the relative merits of particular authors, it is clear that we have at our disposal a vast body of literature that people need to be helped to come to grips with, and that can then yield a mass of insight and suggestion that is not available from any other source.

The argument is that the essence of intelligence lies in grasping the distinction between the empirical and the conceptual, and being able to deal appropriately with either, in understanding the developed traditions of religion, aesthetics, and morality (conceived of in terms of the idea of religion, etc., rather than in terms of any particular religious viewpoint), in understanding mathematical operations, in historical understanding, and in understanding and being well versed in insights into the human condition such as are conveyed in literature. The reason that we can say such understanding constitutes intelligence is that without this range of understanding or without some part of it, the individual will be unable to cope with life in a rational manner. Sooner or later people who lack such understanding will make fools of themselves. If one does have this range of understanding there is no kind of problem that one could not in principle cope with. It is true that particular information is always needed in addition to solve a problem or establish the validity of a claim. But intelligent people are not defined in terms of their stock of information so much as in terms of their ability to assess and utilize information. In that sense, as we have said, intelligence is a process. But it is not to be conceived of in terms of the mysteries of the functioning of the brain. It is defined in terms of one's capacity to understand, which is to be characterized in terms of one's grasp of these fundamental modes of inquiry.

To this point, the characterization of intelligence that I have presented has been couched exclusively in terms of rational capacity. Although there is a contemporary reaction against what is seen by some as too great a preoccupation with rationality, I think that this is broadly as it should be. Other things, such as passion, sincerity, appearance, feel, sense, and intuition may be equally important in themselves, but intelligence is a concept that belongs in the rational camp. The notion of being intelligent and irrational strikes one as contradictory. 'Intelligent' seems the wrong word to describe people who proceed in a non-rational manner, however sane the manner in which they proceed may be thought to be. An intelligent reaction to a problem seems necessarily to imply a thought-out response. One would scarcely attribute intelligence to a person whose pronouncements and actions were not directed by good reason.

However, there is another dimension to intelligence. While the most obvious and ubiquitous characteristic of people whom we regard as intelligent is that, when faced with a problem, they can cope with it rationally in the appropriate manner, intelligence may also be displayed (or not) in making suitable choices, in dealing with other people in appropriate ways, in assessing situations accurately, and in other activities that similarly call for what might colloquially be termed 'insight'. One might, besides, observe that, even when dealing with the rational unravelling of a straightforward intellectual problem, the intelligent person may be marked by a kind of insight that others, by comparison, lack. (This 'insight', so-called, might be thought to bear some relationship to the speed that others have presumed to be an integral part of intelligence.) Sometimes what strikes us most immediately, and what most inclines us to judge people to be intelligent, is that they seem to see to the heart of a complex problem, to focus on what is really significant, and to ignore the irrelevant.[7]

That intelligence should be understood to involve this kind of insight, this element of judgement, or what I should prefer to call this 'imaginative' dimension, is not, I think, in doubt. An intelligent person is not well conceived of purely in terms of rational deliberation and calculation. If only because the term represents such an accolade, we invest the intelligent person with some kind of spark. However, although this is a significant addition to the overall picture, it is to be doubted whether it represents much of a departure from the basically rational overtones of the concept. It is true that we would expect an intelligent person to exhibit imagination (insight, judgement, etc.), but imagination itself is a concept closely bound up with rationality and understanding.

Perhaps popular opinion would have it otherwise. Imagination and insight do tend to be thought of in everyday terms as unique, autonomous modes of awareness. To be imaginative, on such a view, is to be blessed with a kind of self-sufficient and independent sixth sense. Imagination comes to some as a serendipitous visitation, rather as beauty or good eyesight come to some and not to others. But closer reflection will lead us to reject this kind of view entirely. Once again we see the desire to reify and the faith in generic mental abilities at work. But there is no organ, the imagination. There is no thing of any type to correspond to the name. There is only the fact that people may do things in ways which we are pleased to classify as more or less imaginative. And there is no generic capacity to do things imaginatively with which one may or may not be endowed. Imagination, like intelligence itself and other mental concepts we have considered, is closely tied up with understanding and knowledge, and is necessarily contextual. To be imaginative in my story-telling presupposes that I know what I am doing. If a person does something that may be regarded as imaginative in complete ignorance of a situation, then why call the agent imaginative? Why call me an imaginative painter, just because the daubing that I threw off as a joke presents a pattern that others think unusual or pleasing?

Not only does the individual logically have to proceed with understanding to deserve the label imaginative, he or she also has to 'get it right', or produce a response of quality. Whatever its other attributes, we cannot call a response to an economic problem, to a personal problem, or to a call for a work of art, imaginative, if it is absurd, incoherent, inappropriate, or poor in any other way. To be imaginative is indeed to come up with striking and unexpected responses, proposals, or achievements, but they must necessarily be of quality, and the agent must necessarily produce them through understanding rather than by chance. That being so, people may well prove imaginative in some contexts (where they have understanding) and not in others (where they don't).[8]

The intelligent person, then, is indeed to be understood as more than a machine-like creature that, when called upon to do so, can calculate or otherwise reason out the solution to a variety of problems. Intelligent people have understanding, but they also are the kind of people who, because they have understanding, make some decisions, some choices, rather than others. They are, again by definition, relatively imaginative people, but, the nature of imagination being what it is, this means not that they possess some other mysterious generic ability, but that having understanding they are in a position to conceive of good and unusual ideas. Intelligent people are not people with both understanding and imagination. They are enabled to be imaginative by their understanding.

Notes and references

1. John Gingell argues that we could still talk usefully of, e.g., relatively intelligent footballers, circus clowns, and scholars. So we could, but that is to show only that the word 'intelligent' still has utility. It does nothing to refute the point that the concept of intelligence, on these terms, would be too broad to discriminate usefully. (It should be added, for the benefit of my readers who cannot otherwise be expected to know it, that Dr Gingell is not much in sympathy with the idea of a general concept of intelligence anyway. He tends to the view that, while there are common factors that explain why, e.g., we call a particular general and a particular footballer intelligent, there is no particular reason to imagine that there is such a thing as a general notion of intelligence common to both. (Very Wittgensteinian!). I agree with the latter point but then I do not think that the way we use the word 'intelligent' of persons in particular roles (e.g., intelligent footballer) is entirely parallel to the way we use 'intelligence'. Be that as it may, I am not as interested in the question of what it makes sense to assume 'Bobby Charlton was an intelligent footballer' means, as I am in what it makes sense to assume 'Bobby Charlton was an intelligent man' means. Certainly the two can be distinguished. Bobby Charlton may be both an intelligent footballer and an intelligent man. Others may be either one, without necessarily being the other.)

2. I veer between thinking this unproblematic and thinking that it may need further argument. As a back-up to the text, let me first emphasize that I am not making a decisive distinction between rational understanding and, e.g., understanding of people or art. I believe, as I say in the main text, that rational understanding is a large component in understanding art and people. Secondly, I should at least acknowledge that I am aware that it does not seem self-evident to everybody, as it does to me, that appreciation of art, ability to get on with people, empathy with nature, and some form of religious faith are not in themselves relevant to judgements of intelligence.

   Thirdly, this would be a good point at which to refer to Howard Gardner and his theory of multiple intelligences, since to some the thesis represents a middle way between the Scylla of a general notion of intelligence and the Charybdis of a never ending list of specific competencies. To me, unfortunately, it doesn't, since what interests me is the idea of a general notion of intelligence. I do not dispute (I am not in fact in a position to dispute) Gardner's claim that empirical data suggest that individuals may be more or less competent in seven distinct areas, which he calls 'intelligences' (logical-mathematical; linguistic; spatial; bodily-kinaesthetic; musical; interpersonal;

intrapersonal). But this has little to do, for reasons emphasized in the first three chapters, with my interest, which is in the *conceptual* question of whether there seems reason to insist that, e.g., bodily-kinaesthetic or musical ability should be part of the meaning of intelligence. My argument is that the capacity, for instance, to imitate vocal targets, to be sensitive to relative as well as absolute pitch, and to appreciate various kinds of musical pitch, which is what Gardner means by 'musical intelligence', has got little or nothing to do with what I understand by 'an intelligent person'. (See Gardner, H., (1983), *Frames of Mind*, New York: Basic Books.)

3. I did in fact argue just that in Barrow, R., (1976), *Commonsense and the Curriculum*, London: Allen and Unwin, but I now believe that view to be inadequate, for the reasons given above.

4. I have no doubt that some will take exception to this. Is philosophy really so much more clearly defined a field of study than literature? Is science in fact any tidier than either?

5. The emphasis lies on 'in principle'. There are empirical tests (e.g., carbon dating, comparison of sources, air photography) employed by historians, but my point is rather that the logic of a historical claim is such that, if it could be definitively demonstrated, it would be by empirical means.

6. Reference to the need to assess a certain kind of claim through the medium of literature should not be taken to imply that this is the sole function of literature. Nor do I wish to imply that literature is necessarily or even generally written with the conscious aim of elucidating various claims. I do wish to say that there are some human matters concerning which the obvious way to increase one's understanding is by reading literature.

7. Cf. e.g., Bailin, S., (1991), 'Rationality and Intuition', *Paideusis*, 4(2).

8. On imagination, see further Barrow, R., (1988), 'Some observations on the concept of Imagination', in Egan, K. and Nadaner, D., *Imagination and Education*, New York: Teachers College Press.

5. Language, Thought, and Intelligence

Language and Thought

The argument presented so far defines intelligence in terms of mastery or understanding of certain distinguishable developed traditions of inquiry and bodies of thought. Such an account accords very well with the way in which people typically talk about intelligence and make judgements about it; it is also a conception of intelligence that there is good reason to value, and hence it is in accord with the undisputed normative nature of the concept, one that we can intelligibly talk about and make judgements concerning, and one into which we can coherently conduct empirical research, if we choose to do so.

By contrast, the psychological tradition, even leaving aside particular inadequacies in formulation, works with an entirely different kind of conception, in terms of process. That we do judge people's intelligence broadly by reference to their ability to deal with, or 'process', information, rather than in terms of their stock of knowledge or information is not denied. The mistake, if that is the right word, lies in trying to define the concept in terms of the internal workings or processes of the brain, whether tending to the neurophysiological or the metaphorical. We know relatively little about the neurophysiological processes; they are manifestly not what we have in mind when we judge people to be intelligent, and, even if we could identify them in action, they would be of no obvious value except in so far as they were embodied in particular types of understanding. It is not that the brain is activated in a way that indicates the making of connections, for example, that leads us to judge a person to be intelligent. It is a matter of the substantive nature and quality of the connections that are made. Psychological conceptions are not to be dismissed as false so much as largely irrelevant to the educator. Though it is quite obviously true that there are certain neurophysiological goings-on, and that I could be said to be displaying my skills of synthesis, analysis, and problem solving when I proceed intelligently, this is of little educational significance compared with the fact that I will necessarily only be able to exercise intelligence in so far as I have certain kinds of understanding. Furthermore, there is not much educators can do about the student's brain, whereas developing understanding is their primary function. Metaphorical talk about mental processes is even wider of the mark, as metaphorical talk always is.

Intelligence, conceived of in the way I have outlined, could be said to be more or less synonymous with good thinking, in one sense of that phrase. It follows that intelligence not only can be, but actually has to be, developed. To a greater or lesser extent, individuals may be born with brains so constituted as to set limits on what they can hope to achieve (hence the tendency of some psychologists to see intelligence as an innate factor, since their focus is in fact on the neurophysiological conditions necessary to the development of intelligence, rather than on intelligence itself). But, in the vast majority of cases, the degree of intelligence to which people do attain is a product of their learning. (So that there is no misunderstanding, let me reiterate that this is not a contingent fact, but a necessary implication of what we mean by 'understanding'.) The general question of how to develop the capacity to think well (or intelligence) in individuals, therefore, now arises. The argument here will be that, *for all practical purposes* (and that is an important qualification), developing thinking capacity is one and the same thing as developing linguistic capacity. A schooling system that successfully developed in its students a sophisticated command of language would *ipso facto* produce a generation of intelligent people.

The qualification I have drawn attention to indicates at the outset that I do not claim that thinking and using language are identical, or 'isomorphic' as the jargon would have it. The ability to think is not identical with the ability to speak or write. To take an obvious, if extreme, case, an individual might be both mute and physically incapable of writing, but not therefore incapable of thought. A wide variety of social and psychological factors might lead people to think a great deal better than they ever provide evidence of in language.

But does the converse hold? Could a person use language well, whether in spoken or written form, yet not be able to think well? The question might seem to arise because certain individuals speak in ways that impress us, and yet we hesitate to call them intelligent. But, in so far as that is the case, do we not have to presume either that in judging the person to speak impressively we are using different criteria from those that we use when we say that someone thinks well, or that our hesitation to call him intelligent is due to the fact that we do not have evidence that he can think intelligently about things in general? An individual may be said to speak or write well, meaning with charm, fluently, with humour, or other stylistic qualities, and not be presumed to be a good thinker. But that is because good thinking is defined in terms of the quality rather than the style of reasoning, whereas 'speaking well' is here explicitly defined in terms of style. We may say, then, more specifically, that, whereas for a number of reasons a person might think well in the sense of logically, coherently, and clearly, but not be able to speak or write logically, coherently, or clearly, the reverse is not true. In so far as people present us with an oral or written account of something that strikes us as well said in the sense of logical, coherent, and clear, we must presume that they are to that extent good thinkers. (I am ignoring obvious qualifications such as that the account given must be the speakers' own, and not merely a speech they have learned by heart or a line of reasoning with which they have been indoctrinated.)

Evidence that people can speak well on one topic is not in itself sufficient evidence to account them intelligent, since intelligence is a broader concept. People may indeed be knowledgeable and sensible on the subject of, say, painting. But if they cannot display the same qualities when it comes to a debate on aboriginal rights, free trade, or the Second World War, we must assume that their fluency in relation to painting comes from having mastered the debate in the field, rather than from having the broad kind of understanding that characterizes intelligence. For, if they have the latter, they should be able to deal intelligently with other topics, limits on the soundness of their reasoning, conclusions, and pronouncements being set only by lack of information. Thus, intelligent people, while they might produce arguments about free trade or abortion that can legitimately be criticized, because they are ignorant of certain evidence, ought none the less to be able to examine the topic in a coherent and appropriate manner. While it is logically conceivable that a person should be intelligent but unable to speak or write intelligently, that would be a relatively unusual occurrence, and the reverse does not hold at all. But, even if that were not true, we have no way of *judging* whether people think well except by reference to the way they use language, whether in speech or writing. For even seemingly intelligent behaviour or pronouncements cannot reasonably be judged to be so, without knowledge of individuals' reasons for acting as they do or drawing the conclusions that they do.

The conclusion thus seems inescapable that our concern to develop the intelligence of individuals should, in practical terms, manifest itself in a concern to develop their capacity to use language well, in the sense of rationally rather than in the sense of rhetorically or stylistically.

This view about the relationship between language and thought is in my view straightforward common sense.[1] But it needs to be spelt out and asserted, because for some years three popular heresies that involve failure to see it have continued going the rounds. The heresies, which I shall look at individually below, are: first, that there are a number of different types of language to be found in a community and that all are as good as each other; second, that writing is merely one of many modes of expression, comparable to, say, music, painting, or movement; and third, that language and thought are not crucially related, and that consequently intelligence can easily be divorced from being verbally articulate. To set the contrast starkly, the thesis that seems to me plainly correct is that, *with certain obvious exceptions shortly to be noted,* people's thinking capacity is co-extensive with their command of language. Generally speaking, people who habitually speak in a fluent and articulate manner about things, thereby show their intelligence - show that they think fluently and articulately. Conversely, people who speak confusedly, stumblingly, incoherently, and illogically about the main issues of the day or their own problems, thereby, in general, reveal an incapacity to think well.

This must be so, at least in a broad sense, for language is by definition a set of symbols (not necessarily verbal) for expressing thoughts about the world. A highly developed language, such as English, has symbols for abstract ideas as well as concrete things, and also for complicated things like relationships and connections. To understand the word 'because', for instance, is to understand a causal relationship. You don't have to know the English word 'because' in order to appreciate or be aware of that relationship. But you have to have some way of filing it in your mind: you must have this word, some other word or words, some picture, or something. And since what is meant by a language is a set of symbols filed in the mind referring to the outside world, it follows that you must have a language in order to think. It follows also that the more developed and sophisticated the language, the greater the scope for thinking.

It is only a contingent point that for most of us the language in question is verbal. It is logically quite conceivable, and practically quite possible, that some people should operate with a pictorial set of symbols, whereby the symbol is the image of what it symbolizes. But, though that is certainly possible, note how implausible it would be to maintain that somebody brought up in our culture, who shows no signs of having mastered our public language, none the less engages in sophisticated thought in some other, private language. (By a private language is meant a language *all* the terms of which are defined to refer to the private sensations of the user, and whose meanings can therefore be known only to the user. A private language in this technical sense should be distinguished from a personal language, which involves translating the terms of the public language into a secret code.)

It has been argued that the very idea of a private language is logically incoherent.[2] That argument is not important for our purposes. What is important for our purposes is to recognize, first, the enormous improbability of somebody having a private language and yet not sharing the public language to any marked extent. (Of course, if you have the public language, you may also and easily translate it into a personal and secret one. But that possibility causes no problems, since the individual can still communicate through the public language.) Secondly, we need to recognize the poverty that such a language, if it did exist in isolation, would have, unless the individual who spontaneously generated the private language in question happened to be a genius. For it is not just an empty cliché that has it that language is the repository of the wisdom of the ages. That is so in a literal and significant sense - indeed, this is really the crux of the whole issue concerning the importance of language. When new insights about the world are gained, they are perpetuated in language: we learn to talk about camels, jealousy, and atoms only as we come to perceive or conceive them. Conversely, one's language to some extent dictates how one perceives and conceives the world. We gain our knowledge for the most part through our language. We are taught to look at the world in certain ways, and many of those ways, simple as they may seem, would not have been discovered by each one of us individually of our own accord. If people cannot get at the inherited wisdom of the ages through the language in which it is preserved, then they face the monumental task of rediscovering it all for themselves. Thirdly, we must recognize the relative uselessness of a private language, even if one could devise one with a modicum of richness about it. For what is the point of even the deepest of thoughts, if you cannot communicate them to anyone?

The last point, though in itself it constitutes another good reason for valuing public language and ensuring that people gain command of it, goes beyond my immediate concern which is to argue that *in general* people's ability to think is reflected in their use of language. By and large, (private languages being rare and impoverished, if they exist at all) when people cannot articulate a coherent point of view on the breakup of the Soviet Union in a public language, then they haven't got one. Conversely, to enable people to articulate with understanding, or to understand articulate expression, is to increase their power of thought.

The qualifications to this thesis can be summarized in three categories. First, there are various physical impediments, ranging from being mute to having a stammer or a lisp. Then there are psychological impediments represented by shyness in its various manifestations. Thirdly, there are impediments apparently brought about by shortcomings in memory. We might reasonably classify them as physiological impediments. People *do* sometimes know things, have them on the tip of their tongue, but somehow fail to produce them. The argument, then, is not that talk is an index of thought. It is that how one handles language is an index of thought. Whether one handles it publicly or privately is immaterial, so far as this particular point goes. (The reference to private use of public language here should not be confused with the idea of a private language.) For the important thing about the dumb person, the shy person, the person who has temporarily lost a word, is that normally they can handle language, at least in their head. The difference between the shy man and the fool is precisely that the shy man does not do himself justice. It must be admitted, therefore, that we may face a difficult practical problem, when we wish to determine whether people who offer a fairly inarticulate string of remarks about some current issue are shy, lazy, not interested in, or ignorant of the topic, or whether that is the best they can do. But my present purpose is only to stress two points. First, what is meant by 'the best people can do' is, effectively, 'what people can do, at least in their head, regularly enough, when they want to'. Secondly, it is in fact usually reasonably clear whether an individual's performance is being impeded by one or more of the factors noted. By and large, therefore, it remains true that where people consistently fail to express themselves well, that is because they do not think well. The importance of this is twofold; first, negatively, it means that much of the time those who claim that particular individuals are intelligent or clever, despite the fact that they never talk cleverly or intelligently, are talking nonsense. Secondly, positively, it suggests that few things could be more useful in school than to improve children's command of language.

Now this view has been challenged both explicitly and implicitly. First we must look at the claim that there may be many equally valid languages in a community. (The different languages referred to in this context are not generally the traditional 'foreign' languages, so much as sub-species of some dominant language such as English or French.) In extreme form this becomes the claim that there can be no such thing as cultural or linguistic deprivation, because no culture or language can be poor or inferior, measured, as it should be, by its own standards. Thus, working-class language, non-standard Negro English, street language, and academic language are all equally viable alternatives. Such a claim could lead one fairly directly to the view that attempts by schools to improve language skills, at least as usually understood, involve unwarranted attempts to impose unnecessarily a different, but not superior, language on children who already have one.

This line of argument is, however, incredibly confused. Some years ago Basil Bernstein drew a distinction between what he termed elaborated and restricted language codes, the former being more abstract and general in structure, the latter more concrete and particular.[3] He also made the empirical claim that the restricted code was generally to be found amongst the working class, and this, he went on to suggest, often led to a problem of communication between children from such a background and the largely middle-class profession of teachers, using an elaborated code. This fairly simple line of argument seems at times to have been wilfully misunderstood, as if he had said something like 'the working class is ineffably more stupid than the middle class'. And some critics of Bernstein, including followers of Labov,[4] who had carried out field research capturing speech patterns *verbatim*, sought to refute him by arguing that working-class speech had its own distinctive logic and value, in no way inferior to middle-class speech.

But this line of criticism, far from refuting Bernstein, misses the point. Of course different languages or codes may have their own grammatical form and their own values. East End cockney has wit, vivacity, and other distinctive features; measured and dramatic biblical language also has its charms. Nonstandard Negro English certainly isn't just debased, inferior standard English: it is a language with its own grammar and pattern, and its own values. But these various languages are not equally good for any and every purpose. Biblical language comes amiss at the bachelor party; cockney wit is out of place in a court of law. More to the point, if we are concerned with the rational mode of discussion, that is to say with language used primarily to describe and reason with precision, then for that purpose all languages are not equally suited. Nonstandard English is not well equipped for carrying out complex discussion about existentialism, for example, just as formal standard English is rather a portentous language for light banter. The crucial claim that different styles of language may have their own logic is ambiguous, depending on whether by 'logic' we mean grammatical form or logic in the conventional sense. If the former is meant, the claim is of no particular concern for our purposes. The latter claim, to the effect that a syllogism might be valid in standard middle-class English but not in non-standard Negro English, strains one's credulity.

The point that must not be missed about Bernstein's work is that it is logically impossible for the elaborated code to be no better than the restricted code for certain purposes, because this part of the work is a matter of definition. Bernstein *means* by 'an elaborated code' one which is capable of being used to carry on sophisticated abstract discussion; he *means* by 'a restricted code' one less suited to that end. The only part of his thesis that can be challenged is the empirical generalization that by and large working-class children operate with restricted codes.[5] For our present purposes, what needs to be stressed is that there *are* different languages (language codes, sub-languages), but that, though all may have some value of their own and need to be understood on their own terms, some can none the less be clearly seen to be inferior as vehicles for sophisticated, descriptive, analytic, and informative rational thought. There evidently can be linguistic deprivation in the sense that people can lack a species of this particular valuable style of language.[6]

The second objection to be considered is the view that the link between language and thought is not unique. Language, whether spoken or written, it is sometimes claimed, is merely one of many modes of communication, and is exactly on a par with, say, music, painting, movement, or drama. Granted that one could improve people's language skills as a way of improving their thought and expression, one might equally well proceed by improving their painting skills or developing their understanding of movement. This I think is largely wrong, and gains its plausibility from the ambiguity of terms like 'express'.

Music, for example, is obviously 'expressive' in a number of ways. It may 'express' the composer's feelings in the sense of 'be the outcome' of those feelings, it may be said to 'express' the audience's understanding of some broad topic in the sense of represent or evoke feelings, or even thoughts, associated with the topic. But that kind of 'expressing' is decidedly different from that mode of expression which is concerned with carrying an argument or conveying rational understanding. If Mahler's Ninth Symphony is 'about death', that does not mean that it is a contribution to rational thought on the subject of death. As we have said, it may well evoke or convey moods and feelings that people associate with death, it may even cause us to think more deeply about death. But what it is not is a contribution to the intellectual debate about death - what it is, whether it is to be feared, and so on.

One reason for this is very simple: while it could have been otherwise, in point of fact the languages of music, painting, and even to some extent drama, have not been developed in the way that the verbal language has. Musical symbols and conventions are very few, very crude, and not universally recognized, as compared with verbal symbols and conventions. So, while we can and sometimes do create a public language out of sounds, colours, shapes, or movements - we substitute a picture of a hamburger for the word on the cash-register; we use colours and shapes to picture a cat on the mat; we argue that certain chords are melancholy; we move our arms frantically to signal distress - our efforts are crudely representational, extremely limited, and unsophisticated.

It may quite rightly be said, therefore, that the inability to paint or to write music tells you absolutely nothing about a person's capacity for rational thought. But it does not follow that the same goes for people's inability to write or talk. (My argument here, incidentally, besides confirming the point that language and thought are closely linked, must raise some questions about those who seek to defend curriculum time for music, art, and movement studies on the grounds that they contribute to the individual's powers of communication.)[7]

The third heresy with which I have to deal presents the extreme view that my whole thesis is astray and that there is no important link between language and thought. Animals, it may be said, do not have much of a language, but they may still act or think intelligently. In the same way, and going far beyond the qualifications I have already noted, quite ordinary people, untroubled by physical, psychological, and physiological impediments, may be incapable of articulating views, but none the less extremely intelligent. Conversely, many people who converse or write fluently enough may be unintelligent.

Now actually I have little else to say about this view except that it is certainly wrong, as can be seen from what has already been said. The question is: what could anyone who advanced such a thesis possibly mean by 'intelligent behaviour', 'articulate views', or 'good' or 'stupid thinking'? What I understand by intelligent thought is thought that is logical, clear, and reasonably specific; intelligent behaviour is behaviour arising out of intelligent thought. Exactly the same behaviour engaged in at random, though as outsiders we may deem it appropriate or what have you, can hardly be regarded as intelligent. If we observe some unknown animal doing various complicated things apparently intentionally and to good purpose, we say that it seems and very likely is intelligent. But in order for it to proceed intentionally, it has to engage in thinking with some set of symbols, some language. If we insist that it has no language, then it cannot proceed intentionally, and if it cannot proceed intentionally then it cannot be acting intelligently.[8] Similarly, if a person is incapable of explaining coherently why he supports Bill Clinton or John Major, and this is not because he is shy, mute, bored, or such like, but because he lacks the verbal wherewithal, then why on earth should we classify his position as intelligent? Why, when faced with people who generally cannot give an account of themselves in words and who we have no reason to suppose can give an account of themselves in any other way, should we want to say that they are, or might none the less be, intelligent? Conversely, if we are faced with people who, whatever we think of them and whatever their failings in other respects, can articulate coherent arguments, can provide reasoned support for their behaviour and views, how can we deny that they are intelligent, for that is more or less what intelligence means?

Intelligence, Education, and Traditions of Thought

Let me summarize in some detail the argument of Part I.

Schooling is appropriately concerned with many things, including the socialization, moral development, physical fitness, and, perhaps, vocational guidance of children. Such matters are generally thought to be of importance from the point of view of both the individual and society as a whole. But schooling is centrally about education: we provide a public system and invest considerable resources in that system and in the education of teachers, in order, primarily, to provide equal educational opportunity for all individuals, regardless of their private circumstances and apparent talents, limitations, and interests at the outset, again for the presumed good of both the individual and society. We believe, with good reason, that through education the individual may become more fully developed, entering more fully into a specifically human way of life, and that society, particularly a society founded on liberal democratic principles, will function considerably more successfully with educated citizens.

Education in turn is centrally about developing understanding. It is concerned with developing the mind rather than the body, and is focused on such things as comprehension, discernment, appreciation, insight, and awareness in relation to ideas, judgements, beliefs, and the like, rather than on such things as developing particular physical skills, inculcating manners and modes of behaviour, or providing emotional security. This is not to say that these other matters are of no interest to teachers. Of course they are, partly because, as has already been said, the school has come to take on wider responsibilities than education alone (e.g., socialization), partly because some skills, some security, some degree of physical fitness, and so on, are necessary foundations for, and elements in, successful education (e.g., the ability to read, a degree of confidence), and partly because ultimately these various concepts are interrelated (e.g., notions such as creativity, imagination, and moral responsibility necessarily involve a considerable degree of understanding). But it is to say that the business of education as such is the business of developing understanding. The importance of understanding lies partly in the fact that it is a peculiarly human achievement - other animals learn things and can be trained, but they do not acquire understanding - and thus makes us more fully human, partly in that it contributes to our development in other areas such as the affective, the moral, and the aesthetic, and partly in that it gives individuals greater control over their destinies, more scope for choice, and in that a greater understanding spread more widely through the population gives us collectively more chance of coping with problems, more chance of living prosperous and happy lives in harmony with each other, and more chance of creating a future in accordance with our wishes and needs.

When, therefore, we encounter attempts to make such concepts as self-esteem, the child's expressed interests, creative self-expression, citizenship, basic skills, vocational training, or emotional security the focus of the school curriculum, we must object. Not because these are unimportant matters, not because they should not be in some way a concern of the school, but because they are subsidiary to the prime purpose of the school which is to *educate* in the sense of develop the mind by building up understanding. To build up self-esteem, for instance, is neither the prime purpose of the school system, nor even desirable, if, for example, that self-esteem happens to be based upon ignorance, crudity, and a lack of respect for others, as it well might be. The only kind of self-esteem that is ultimately worthy of respect is a proper sense of one's own worth based upon a reasonable understanding of the world and people within it. Thus, a reasonable self-esteem may be a legitimate and valuable by-product of education, and some concern for self-esteem may be an important means to successful education along the way, but it is not a defining characteristic of education, and its importance has to be judged in relation to the primary goal of developing understanding.

The analysis of education in terms of understanding can be disputed. This is because, as has been emphasized, concepts, at least of the complex abstract kind, cannot be definitively defined in an indisputably correct way *(see pp. 37- 41)*. If a person conceives of education as nothing more than what the rest of us would call socialization, or if he maintains that it is to be defined in terms of self-esteem, it is inappropriate to say in either case that he is mistaken or that the definition is incorrect or false. The appropriate thing to say is, first, that on a purely verbal level these two views of education certainly involve unusual, even idiosyncratic, uses of the word (at this level one might even talk of 'incorrect' use of the word, since there are at any given time certain conventions governing the use of words); but secondly, and more importantly, one may say that these alternative conceptions of education are not our concern, for the sorts of reason given above: we value education in another sense a great deal more. One might take the time to explore one or both of these alternative conceptions, to see whether the person putting them forward can explain them adequately, meeting the criteria of clarity, coherence, completeness, and compatibility; but, in as much as nobody to my knowledge has produced an adequate (by these criteria) analysis in terms of socialization or self-esteem, it seems probable that the individual in question would fail to make his case, being in some way guilty of confusion, incomprehensibility, inconsistency, self-contradiction, incompleteness, or incompatibility. But if we do not have the time to take the long way round, or if the proponent of some other view is unwilling to defend it in this manner, we must revert to the direct challenge relating to value. What is there to be said in favour of education, if it means simply socialization or the promotion of self-esteem? Is there any good reason to want our schools to concentrate on education in either of these senses rather than in the sense of developing understanding? The answer would appear to be *no*. Not only is the conception in terms of understanding relatively clear, coherent, consistent, fully articulated, and compatible with our broader view of things, in particular our values, it is also a view of education that we have an interest in defending. Putting it crudely: socializing children is not enough, promoting their self-esteem is not enough, (and both are to be positively deplored, if done on any terms), while developing their understanding is a goal to be highly prized. As we have said, it is the key to the individual's self-fulfilment, to control of our individual and collective destiny, and to a reasonable and morally acceptable society. The attempt to provide understanding will not guarantee success in any of these respects, but it is what we need to do if we value such goals.

We presume, then, that good reason has been given to champion education in the sense of developing understanding. Now, for a long time the word 'intelligence' has played a prominent part in educational discourse. Its prominence is due partly to the fact that education is generally conceived of as being an intellectual or cognitive business, and partly to the fact that 'intelligence' is our key normative term for referring to people's broad quality of mind, as opposed to particular expertise or abilities. Since 'intelligence', at the level of a dictionary definition, refers to our capacity to understand, and since education (for most of us) is centrally concerned with developing understanding, it is not surprising that intelligence is a key word in the vocabulary of education.

A major problem has arisen, however, because the concept has not been properly analysed by educationalists (and such analysis as has been provided by philosophers has been largely ignored).[9] A paradoxical consequence has been that, notwithstanding the strong conceptual link between education and intelligence, a notion of intelligence has gained ground in educational circles that more or less divorces it from the kind of understanding that is characteristic of education. The concept of intelligence, as educational psychologists in particular tend to conceive it, is inadequately analysed, but it is taken none the less to suggest that we are dealing with some kind of innate mechanism that is related to understanding while at the same time being divorced from any substantive understanding. In general terms, the lack of clear analysis means that we claim to be researching intelligence, to be assessing it in individuals, to be looking out for it as teachers, to be utilizing it, and to be developing it, without agreeing, and in some cases without apparently knowing, what it is. More specifically, some working definitions of intelligence amongst researchers would appear to make it something of no obvious educational value (e.g., the ability to score well on an IQ test), and others involve presuppositions of a highly questionable nature, most notably the idea that there is some general innate capacity or set of generic skills. Not only are these definitions in terms of some general ability questionable, they also seem to lack educational significance, since we can neither identify them accurately nor conclude that such ability, if it exists, sets any clear limits on what an individual could hope to achieve in terms of mental development. If the case were otherwise, we might be able to say something like, 'This student has this degree of intelligence and as a result will be able to cope with x, but will never be able to cope with y', and that would be of some service to teachers. But in point of fact we cannot identify and quantify these alleged general skills in any systematic or plausible way, let alone accurately. And we have every reason to suppose that, by and large, in general, even if they exist, they set no clear limits on what an individual might hope to achieve. Once again, putting it crudely: a teacher would have no good reason to conclude that a student could or could not become an impressive historian, a significant scientist, a wonderful poet, a leading psychologist, or a good and successful politician, from any of the typical research findings about intelligence. The psychologists' approach to intelligence does not enable us to predict very much about individuals on its own terms, and its terms are anyway of little educational interest, since we do not have any particular reason for caring whether they can improve their scores on standardized tests.

This being the case, we need to articulate a conception of intelligence that meets the criteria of sound analysis, which is to say that is clear, complete, coherent, and compatible, and that does justice to logical restraints and the facts as they seem to be, and that is relevant to our educational concerns and values. (If we cannot do the last consistently with the first two, we should have to conclude, admittedly with some surprise, that intelligence was not a concept of particular educational interest. But, as it happens, and as is to be expected given the superficial meanings of the terms, it can be done.)

Such an articulation of the concept of intelligence can be provided in terms of broad understanding of certain distinguishable kinds of question and related traditions of inquiry and bodies of thought. An intelligent person, by definition, is capable of displaying his mental capability across a broad spectrum, and is not to be identified with a person who simply has considerable expertise in a particular area. But this does not mean that we should conceptualize intelligence in terms of process or a set of generic skills. That approach is to be rejected because it does not ultimately make sense, since the idea of a capacity divorced from substantive understanding or a content is not coherent. What it means is that we must conceptualize intelligence in terms of combined capabilities to understand various particular contents. If we can find an economic way to describe the various important kinds of understanding there are, which collectively would enable a person to cope appropriately with any kind of problem, provided that they had access to relevant information, then we should have succeeded in defining intelligence. (The need for it to be economic or manageable arises because we hope that the concept will be useful. If in the event we feel we can only define intelligence in terms of, say, the itemization of all the things that there are to be understood, from baseball to botulism, we would have a comprehensible conception, but one that was far too general and diffuse to serve any particular purpose. The meaning of 'good', for example, is at one level clear enough, but it is such a general term as to provide little assistance to us as a way of classifying or making judgements.)

It has been argued, in the light of the above considerations, that an intelligent person is one who can distinguish, recognize, and deal appropriately with dimensions to a question, claim, or problem, that are, variously, empirical, conceptual, aesthetic, moral, mathematical, historical, religious, and interpersonal. It is not denied that there are various other coherent ways of categorizing and classifying understanding, nor, therefore, that in one sense one may refer to a 'political' or 'sociological' problem as readily as an 'aesthetic' or 'historical' one. The argument is that the classification provided is logically more fundamental: a political problem may have conceptual, historical or empirical dimensions, but there is no such thing as a distinguishable political dimension (beyond its subject matter). By contrast the notion of an empirical dimension cannot be usefully further subdivided.

Developing intelligence by some means or other (which is thus seen to be not only possible but actually necessary) is, therefore, in broad terms, a matter of providing such understanding. The heavy cognitive or rational stress of this account of intelligence is not a matter for apology: intelligence is, if ever a concept was, a largely cognitive matter. The opposition that this sometimes engenders may be presumed to be the result of a fear that we emphasize the intellectual at the expense of other human qualities such as feelings and emotions. But to insist that intelligence is a cognitive matter is not to deny the importance of other values. It is simply to point out that this particular concept does not directly incorporate other things that we value. Besides, as has been explained, though intelligence is not to be defined in terms of such things as imagination, it has considerable relevance to the development of such a quality. You do not have to be imaginative to be intelligent, but you cannot be imaginative to any noteworthy degree if you lack intelligence.

Since in practice one's intelligence is co-extensive with one's capacity to handle public verbal language, one way of characterizing education would be as, 'the initiation of the individual into the public language and the subsequent development of a sophisticated command of that language including the specialist languages' that have been referred to. Arguments about the possible value of alternatives to the public verbal language, be they non-public verbal or non-verbal languages, are largely irrelevant. This debate takes place within the context of the public verbal language. It is intelligence in that context with which we are concerned. Certainly, a culture with quite different understanding of the world would judge people's intelligence in a different way. But in our culture, which means the culture of anyone who can understand this book, even if they do not agree with all of its argument, science is an identifiable activity and is to be distinguished from witchcraft, morality is a central concept and is to be distinguished from religion, the conceptual and the empirical are to be distinguished, the aesthetic needs to be understood on its own terms, and the works of a Nietzsche, even though in the judgement of some they may be obscure, are to be distinguished from the ravings of a Hitler.[10] There is undeniably, therefore, both a culturally specific element in this analysis of intelligence, as in any other, and an element that takes guidance from the collective wisdom of tradition. It is difficult to see how it could be otherwise, or why we should wish to set ourselves against our culture and the inherited understanding and wisdom of tradition.   And, of course, if tomorrow we become convinced that we have got it wrong and that witchcraft is another kind of understanding, we should modify our conception of intelligence accordingly. In the meantime, the understanding that constitutes intelligence must be taken to be the understanding that has the broad acceptance of those who study such things and that governs our world. It is the understanding enshrined in the public language and housed in our minds and in the world's major written works. That we may disagree about the merits of a Shakespeare, a Shaw, a Hawking, or a Hanfling is neither here nor there. Intelligent people are those who can get to grips with such thinkers and argue about their respective merits.

Notes and references

1. The rest of this section draws on my argument in Barrow, R., (1982), *Language and Thought: Rethinking Language Across the Curriculum*, London, Ontario: Althouse Press, a book originally only available in Canada and now out of print.
2. See, for example, Jones, O.R. (ed.), (1970), *The Private Language Argument*, London: Macmillan.
3. Bernstein, B.B., (1971-3), *Class, Codes and Control*, 3 vols, London: Routledge and Kegan Paul.
4. Labov, W., (1966 and 1969), *The Social Stratification of English in New York City*, Washington DC: Center for Applied Linguistics, and Champaign, Ill.: NCTE.
5. The above should not be read as a wholehearted endorsement of Bernstein's thesis. I refer to his work merely to make the point that empirical evidence could be produced to show that some languages are by their nature more suited to particular tasks than others.
6. It may be asked why, if it is conceded that some different languages may be equally appropriate for certain tasks, and some good for some things, others for others, I believe it to be educationally desirable to focus on only one (type of) language. This is an important question, the answer to which takes us to the heart of the fundamental value issues that I attempt to address in Part Two. In outline, I suggest that one supremely important value in the cultural tradition that I both belong to and value is intelligent communication of the sort I am attempting to analyze. I also suggest that there are good reasons for us all to value this and that most of those who read this book do in fact value it (no doubt amongst a wider variety of other things), though they may not hitherto have consciously acknowledged it. For the purposes of intelligent communication in a society it is necessary that all have access to a shared language that has the requisite features.
7. This is the issue referred to in the Preface that elicited concerned comment from more than one of my readers. Both Sharon Bailin and John Gingell, perhaps not surprisingly given their expertise and interest in the arts, object, suggesting essentially that I have just got it wrong. The arts, they say, also involve complex symbolic systems, which are not cruder so much as different. The differences include i) that they do not seek to convey or analyze propositional knowledge to the same extent or in the same way as the verbal language, ii) that their symbols are often more

ambiguous, which may be a virtue, and iii) that the kind of understanding provided by the novelist or painter adds flesh to the skeleton provided by philosophic understanding.

I agree. There are such differences and they are extremely (for all I say to the contrary, equally) important. But surely this does not invalidate what I say in the previous note and what is part of the burden of the main text: if you want to communicate a crucial and central chunk of human understanding, or understand it, there is no substitute for mastering the verbal language.

Please note that I say only that 'the inability to paint or write music tells you absolutely nothing about a person's capacity for rational thought'. I do not say that the converse is true, preferring to avoid that question, having rather a lot of other things on my plate!

8. I have used a similar argument before and been wrongly interpreted to have denied that animals have intelligence. Please note that I have not said anything about whether animals do or do not possess intelligence.

9. See, for example, Kleinig, J., (1982), *Philosophical Issues in Education*, New York: St. Martin's Press; Glover, J. (ed.), (1976), *The Philosophy of Mind*, Oxford: Oxford University Press; Gustafson, D.F. (ed.), (1967), *Essays in Philosophical Psychology*, London: Macmillan.

10. Even within 'our' culture there are arguments about all my examples. That does not alter the fact that a description of 'our' culture would have to incorporate these assumptions. The onus would be on an individual who wanted to teach that science and witchcraft were indistinguishable to convince others.

PART II
Education

6. Value Judgements

Values and Objectivity

Throughout Part I, I have made explicit reference to values. One of my implicit themes is that it is the value questions that are crucial to, and are being largely ignored in, educational theory generally. An explicit theme has been that intelligence is a value-loaded term, and that therefore its definition must be partly determined by what kind of understanding we value. There is no escaping this. At the same time, I have necessarily involved myself with substantive value judgements, arguing, for instance, that we should value historical understanding more than the ability to do crossword puzzles or to achieve a high score on an IQ test. As I say, I have attempted to argue and give reasons to support some of these judgements, rather than merely asserted or assumed their validity. But at this point it would be prudent to give consideration to a popular view to the effect that value judgements are no more than a matter of taste. In the end, it may be said, we get down to the fact that a particular author thinks it worthwhile for people to study history, philosophy, and so forth. That opinion is of no more significance than the fact that he also values opera, country-and-western music, and sugar in his tea. Nothing can be said to show that those of us who have very different values and tastes should change them. Therefore we will continue to concentrate on the self-esteem of our children, to take their IQ scores seriously, or whatever.

The view that value judgements are not really judgements in any sense, but just a matter of arbitrary opinion, is one of the most damaging views to have affected education in the last two decades. It is damaging because, if taken seriously, it inevitably leads to the conclusion that it doesn't matter what we do, not to mention the fact that it would justify (or excuse) what one would otherwise characterize as pernicious and horrific educational practices. For, all decisions about what to do, even when they are primarily questions about means, involve some reference to ends, whether it is made explicit or not. The claim that a certain style of teaching, for example, is superior to others, can only be reasonably made in the light of both empirical evidence that it has certain consequences and an evaluative claim to the effect that such consequences are

89

desirable. So, if the ends that we value are just a matter of taste, not only will we have no way to choose between the different ends that are variously proposed, we will also lose any reason to object to any particular means or practice: a particular practice may be shown to lead to a particular result, but, since no result is to be preferred to another except in terms of an individual's fancy, there is no reason to be concerned that this policy was adopted rather than that. Every policy will suit some end or other, and all ends have equal validity. To worry about what was going on in a particular school would be as pointless as worrying about the fact that some people like detective stories.

In fact, of course, proponents of such a view are seldom, if ever, consistent. That is to say, whatever they claim to believe, they are sooner or later to be found objecting to some particular value judgement as if it were indefensible or outrageous in some objective way.[1] They say it is just a matter of opinion, but they do not think it acceptable to hold the opinion that the indoctrination practised in the schools in Hitler's Germany, the apartheid reinforced in South African schools, or the scientific nonsense taught in the name of Lysenko in Soviet schools was legitimate. We can be thankful that there are limits to the opinions that they regard as justifiable, but it is confusing, to say the least, to discover that they do not in fact mean what they say. It is not just a matter of opinion: it is at the very least a matter of opinion within some (unspecified) limits. In some cases, they seem clearly, if unwittingly, to trade upon the degree of consensus afforded by a given community or culture. Thus they mean, more specifically, something such as, 'given that in this society none of us is going to value the end of promulgating manifest nonsense or obvious evil, within the broad area of socially acceptable values my opinion is as good as yours'. That is rather different, and might conceivably be true, although I shall argue below that it is not.

Quite apart from the fact that few people, if any, actually do consistently believe that values are just a matter of taste, such a view is in any case incoherent. It is never the case within a particular sphere of activity that any value judgement is as good as any other, and it could not be the case, because any activity that is recognizable as being a certain kind of activity rather than another is necessarily defined in certain terms, which automatically set limits on intelligible value judgements in the area. Cooking is distinguishable from singing, driving, nuclear physics, and a host of other activities. Because of what cooking is - something to do, I suppose, with preparing food in a hygienic, tasty, and delectable way - there are certain judgements that do, and others that do not, make sense. I, for example, am a very bad cook: I know next to nothing about it, could care less, and really would not know how to prepare anything from a reasonable steak and kidney pie to a soufflé. Given those facts, it is plainly a matter of objective truth (by which is meant, in this context, something demonstrable by public criteria that go way beyond any individual's mere taste) that I am a poor cook. Even if, by some strange quirk of taste, you happen to like the mess I serve up, we should not be inclined to say that in your judgement I am a good cook. Cooking is, like all others, a public concept. Given what cooking means in our culture, I am not a good one, and we should rather say that you do not mind the fact that I am a bad cook. Because of what soccer is, because of its constituent rules, the objectives of the game and so on, it is a matter of objective judgement, rather than mere individual opinion, that Pelé was a great soccer player. It is not just chance that many fans of the game happen to share this taste for Pelé: it is because they understand the game that they can see the evidence that shows that he was a great player. In exactly the same way, what constitutes good educational practice is to a large extent determined by the nature of education.

Admittedly, the nature of education, what education is about, is more debatable than what cooking or soccer are about. Furthermore, while one can show that some judgements about who is and who is not a good soccer player are absurd, it is the case that some judgements may be debatable (e.g., 'Pelé was a better soccer player than Cruyff'), and that making judgements about the relative value of quite distinct activities (e.g., cooking and soccer) is considerably more problematic. These three points - contentious judgements within an activity, relative judgements about activities, and varying degrees of contestability among concepts - therefore need to be considered.

The fact that some judgements within an activity are fine ones and may not be satisfactorily resolvable need not detain us long. If in the end we cannot objectively establish the superiority of Pelé over Cruyff, or vice versa, it is of very little moment, as it would be if we could not finally establish whether Bertrand Russell was a better or worse philosopher than Wittgenstein. We can easily enough live with those kinds of disagreement, and even concede that at this level differing judgements may boil down to a matter of taste, provided we recognize that this does not alter the objectivity of the judgements that both Pelé and Cruyff were good soccer players, and both Russell and Wittgenstein good philosophers.

As to the question of whether it is better to be educated or to be a good soccer player or a good cook, we can concede straightaway that the question cannot be answered in any meaningful way, if it is not further qualified by reference to some overarching concern or set of purposes. That is to say, the unadorned and unqualified judgement that it is better to be a good soccer player than a good cook had best be left to stand as an expression of taste. But the matter is very different if the question is raised in some context, such as better for purposes of self-satisfaction, better for purposes of making money, of receiving adulation, of finding other related interests, of exercising one's mind, and so on. It doesn't matter what the answer may be in such cases, nor that in some cases it will be hard, perhaps impossible, to arrive at a certain answer. The point is that when activities are being compared in respect of value, objective considerations do come into play provided the comparison is made in reference to some particular concern(s) or purpose(s). In that case the concern or purpose provides the criteria in terms of which the activities have to be judged. So, while it means little to say that being educated is better than being a good soccer player, it certainly means something to suggest that it is more valuable if you want to be fully developed as a human being, or if you want to be a relatively autonomous individual with some control over your destiny, or if you want to understand the world. Not only does it mean something, in these particular cases the judgement can be readily enough shown to be objectively reasonable, because of the connection between what we mean by education and what we mean by such things as being a fully developed human being.

The point that a concept such as education is more debatable than the concept of soccer is the most interesting of the three points raised here, from a philosophical point of view. It is true; and, given that people may reasonably argue about what constitutes being educated, does it not follow that within this sphere at any rate we cannot make objective value judgements? If one person thinks that being educated is largely a matter of amassing a store of information (facts and figures), another that it is a matter of feeling good about yourself, another that it is a matter of being a good critical-thinker, and another a matter of acquiring the sort of understanding I have outlined, they are inevitably going to make quite different particular judgements about the extent to which various individuals are well educated. How are we going to decide between them in some objective manner? Will it not truly be a matter of individual taste, deriving in each case from a different conception of education?

Well, it will of course, but this is to ignore the point that, while the concept of education is more debatable than the concept of soccer, as we have repeatedly said, it is not a matter of arbitrary whim. There are rules to be followed in analysing this or any other concept, and while in a case such as this the rules do not force one to accept a particular conception as the correct one or as the truth, they do force one to reject some conceptions on the grounds that they are unclear, inconsistent, incoherent or incompatible with what we know (or believe) about people and the world in general. If we are trying to talk about 'education', we also have to start from some point of contact with the word as conventionally defined. Reason, evidence, and argument, therefore, still play a large part in the process. It is an empirical question, but it is doubtful whether, if we all played scrupulously by the rules of analysis, we would in fact end up with very different conceptions of education. But, in so far as we did, in so far, in other words, as what you and I meant by 'education', and therefore what we were trying to achieve with children, was significantly different, we still would not be reduced to mere preference, idle whim, or arbitrary judgement. There is still scope for reasoned argument, taking account of logic and evidence, as to which conception of education has more merit in what respects. To put it oversimply: it is not the case that whether you want the next generation of children to be educated in the sense of given broad understanding is a matter of taste, akin to whether you enjoy detective stories or science fiction. There are reasons to be given and assessed in the light of other values and opinions we have, which may themselves need to be, and to some extent can be, rationally assessed. Coming to a conclusion on this issue is a rational rather than an arbitrary process.

What some of the reasons are for valuing the conception of education I have put forward has already been indicated in previous pages. To some extent there is an issue of good faith or sincerity here, as well. For while it is possible to argue about the values being endorsed in these pages - to question, perhaps, some of the reasoning, to discredit some of the evidence or introduce different evidence, and to dissent from some of the value judgements - it is worth considering whether all the objections that might be put forward could be sincere objections.

The phenomenon of abstract argument designed to show that a case has not been fully made is an important aspect of our culture. But sometimes, when we are concerned ultimately with the need for action of some sort, as we are in the field of education, it is necessary to distinguish carefully between a verdict of 'not proven definitively', and a verdict to the effect that a practice should not be engaged in. Hence, one question worth asking is: does anybody seriously believe that lack of understanding of the type specified would be a good thing? In other words, let us clearly distinguish between the suggestion that the argument given above might be challenged in various ways (which is certainly the case) and the suggestion that the conclusion deserves to be substantially rejected.

Without question, some people do want to reject (and historically have rejected) the conclusion that schools ought to provide education in the sense I have outlined. Some, for example, believe that we ought to follow the dictates of the Lord in an uncritical manner or in some other form of received wisdom such as party ideology. Some nations and groups have provided education in this sense. But, such views can themselves be, and indeed have been, challenged very effectively. Which religious view is supposed to have a monopoly on truth?

How in any particular case do we know that the received wisdom is worthy of respect? Do we not deny a fundamental aspect of being human, if we surrender our critical faculties? If true understanding is not something that we can achieve for ourselves, how are we to know that a given ideology or religious view represents true understanding? Such questions serve to highlight the genuinely arbitrary and non-rational nature of preferring acquiescence in received wisdom to some form of autonomous and rational self-direction. One may add that lack of understanding leads all too readily to misunderstanding, and that, historically, ideologically driven communities do not inspire much confidence. But rather than pursue in detail an argument designed to show the inadequacy of the case for not developing critical understanding in individuals, at this juncture I raise the different question of whether any reader of this book does sincerely believe that it would be better for us not to examine issues for ourselves, whether any reader seriously maintains that we would be better off if we did not attempt to understand how it is that aeroplanes fly, what it is that musicians and other artists have attempted to do over the centuries, the problems inherent in religious claims, the insights provided by writers, the history of mankind, the dangers of unhygienic conditions, the way in which to set a broken limb, the nature of morality, and the potential of technological innovation.

I suggest that as a matter of fact the vast majority of us do believe in the value of such understanding. If that is indeed so, the point being made here is that we must guard very carefully against allowing our admirable commitment to abstract argument to lead us to the conclusion that we have no reason to value what in fact we do value. The mere fact that we do value such understanding is itself a reason for valuing it, if subjectivism is true. If the extreme view that such a value judgement was necessarily entirely arbitrary were true, it would presumably be in order to observe that in that case a majority commitment to a set of values was as good a reason as any other for the dominance of those values in a community (and would in practice inevitably settle the issue anyway). Where there is no room for reason, there is no scope for complaining about the unreasonableness of the dominant opinions.

But, in point of fact, as I have indicated, there *are* reasons to value such understanding, essentially in that it gives us access to the various types of achievement we have produced, it gives us a measure of control over our lives, it allows us to live to a certain degree in a predictable world, it makes us more fully human, it provides us with a multiplicity of sources of interest and pleasure, and it puts us in a stronger position to cope with changing circumstances. All of that remains true, even if some would be reluctant to add, as I would not, that we are also in a position to come nearer to the truth, which is a good in itself.

Elitism

So, on the assumption that there is value in the idea of education conceived of as the development of understanding, that that understanding can be categorized in terms of eight basic developed traditions of study *(see pp. 58 - 60)*, that such understanding can be equated with the kind of intelligence we are interested in as educators, and that developing such understanding can be equated with developing the individual's linguistic capacity, we ask what this means in practice and in more detail for schooling. What does it mean for the practical business of organizing the school curriculum and for teaching? What do we need to do to ensure that we have done all that we could reasonably do to cultivate the intelligence of our students? Are we already doing the right kind of thing, or are we moving away from the goal of cultivating intelligence, either because we no longer value it, or because we are inadvertently doing the wrong kind of thing to achieve that goal? I shall begin by repudiating some common misapprehensions.

First of all, it does not necessarily mean a reversion to (or a continuation of) the familiar subject-based curriculum as traditionally taught. There has been persistent and widespread misunderstanding on this point, some critics being content with an emotive dismissal of the whole argument as 'élitist', 'old-fashioned', and 'self-serving' (the last on the grounds that those who hold such a view can sometimes be seen to have been the beneficiaries of some such educational experience). Such criticism, alas, is self-serving in its own way, and it betrays the lack of understanding that we need to guard against. For, one of the most basic fallacies in logic is the *ad hominem* argument: the type of argument that inappropriately tries to discredit what is said by discrediting the character or motives of the presenter of the argument. It may be true, as a generalization, that people are inclined to espouse that with which they are familiar, but it is obviously not always true. And in any case the fact that the champion of, say, a particular religion may happen to be a believer brought up in the faith obviously has no logical bearing on the quality of his argument. In the same way, the question of who did or did not experience an education along the lines advocated here has got nothing to do with the argument about its desirability.

Similarly, to castigate it as 'old-fashioned' is neither here nor there. Many of our most profound moral views are very old-fashioned indeed, as are the institution of marriage and certain basic geometric truths. Perhaps, indeed, some of these old-fashioned views should be rejected, but if so, it will not be because they are old-fashioned, but because we have reason to reject them as inadequate. There is nothing necessarily good about novelty, innovation, or change. The value of this or any other educational proposal has to be assessed by reference to the argument, not to its degree of familiarity. (I am reminded of the insane crusade against the Four Olds - old thought, old habits, old culture, old customs - conducted by the Red Guards in Mao Zedong's China).[2]

The charge that the kind of proposal I am putting forward is élitist is more interesting, despite the fact that in some cases it is obviously related to the suggestion that it is self-serving. There are two issues here: the question of whether it is élitist, and the question of whether, if it is, that is necessarily objectionable. The claim that it is élitist may be based upon the view that what is being advocated is something akin to the type of schooling provided by the English grammar school, particularly in the decade or so following the Second World War (and for a much longer period by the British public, i.e., private, schools). As a matter of fact, as we shall see in a moment, this is by no means necessarily the case. But it is also questionable whether that type of curriculum, as opposed to the system of education of which it was a part, was élitist. Since, at the period in question, the English system of education involved three different types of school (the grammar, the secondary modern, and the technical), and since there was a fairly positive correlation between the social background of individuals and the type of school they went to, and since the type of schooling they received also correlated fairly highly with the kinds of job they ultimately went into, there is a case for saying that the system was élitist. By and large, the children of the well-to-do received a grammar school education and moved on to more prosperous kinds of employment. I will not comment further on this, since, as I say, it is an issue to do with the system of schooling, which is not my present concern, rather than the nature of the curriculum. But I cannot forbear noting that, ironically, the instrument of selection for the grammar school (the eleven-plus examination) bore a marked resemblance to a set of standardized achievement tests, including what was essentially a test of IQ. In other words, to some extent, the system was justified and maintained by a belief in intelligence as some generic innate capacity, of the type that I have argued strongly against.

But it is also believed by some that the grammar school curriculum was inherently élitist, on the grounds that it was only suited to a certain type of student. This concern shades into the further question of whether élitism is necessarily objectionable. If it were the case that a certain kind of curriculum was only suited to some, should it therefore be rejected? But before considering that, it is important to point out that there is not really any evidence to support or deny the claim that the grammar school curriculum was only suited to some. The selection procedure was not necessarily, and certainly was never shown to be, an adequate way of determining an individual's suitability to the curriculum in question. Those who went into either of the alternative types of school were so rapidly caught up in a different kind of experience that it remains largely unknown how they would have fared had they gone to a grammar school (notwithstanding the fact that a small number of individuals did successfully transfer at a later age). The point being made here is that we have no real evidence to set against the suggestion that the vast majority of students could cope very successfully with a grammar school-type curriculum, the more so if we add that the precise form of such a curriculum and the manner of teaching it might well be markedly different from the historical example we are here considering. In fact, the conviction that many could not benefit from such a curriculum seems itself to be a form of élitism (and perhaps a far more pernicious form), for it seems that it must be based upon the idea that some are innately more gifted than others. While I have never denied in these pages that there does seem to be good reason to accept that different individuals may to some extent be born with, or very rapidly acquire, limits to what they can achieve, it is a claim of the argument I have put forward that to a very large extent the kind of intelligence that we ought to be concerned about is a product of learning, rather than a given commodity which determines our chances of learning. We are in no position to claim that a certain individual has such and such a potential to master historical understanding. We are in a position to say that, if we do certain things with an individual, we are very likely to develop historical understanding.

It is by no means clear, then, that developing the kind of understanding we are concerned with is suitable only for a privileged minority. But, if it were, would there be any reason to object? 'Elitist' has become a pejorative word, there is no denying, but the question arises as to what descriptive meaning should be given to the term to justify the negative implications. If 'élitist' means something like 'a situation in which preferential treatment or special regard is given to people in virtue of their wealth, power, or class' it may well be objectionable. But if it is, it is objectionable because factors such as wealth, power, and class can be argued to be irrelevant reasons for giving people preferential treatment. If, by contrast, we were to give musical instruments to the musically gifted, places in a soccer team to the better players, or managerial office to the more competent, it is difficult to see what the objection could reasonably be. At a given point in time, some people are better at doing some things than others, and in many, if not all, cases that seems an excellent reason for deciding that those with the appropriate talent should engage in the activity in question. The proposal before us, if it were the case that only some people could benefit from this particular kind of education, involves so-called élitism only in this second and unobjectionable sense: providing a desirable education to those who are capable of benefiting from it. It is only the politics of envy that would deny a certain valued kind of education (or more generally, way of life) to all, solely on the grounds that some could not benefit from it. And the politics of envy is a sure-fire prescription for mediocrity and ultimately collapse. But, in any case, as we have seen it, is highly debatable whether it is true that only a minority are capable of successfully undertaking such an education.

To return to the question of what the curriculum implications of the argument are, it is not in fact the case that what is proposed amounts to a carbon copy of some stereotype of the grammar school curriculum as was, anyway. To establish logical distinctions between certain theoretically distinguishable subjects, and to argue further that people need to be aware of these distinctions and to be capable of engaging with each of these subjects, is in itself to say absolutely nothing about how a curriculum that covers this ground should be either organized or taught. I do not intend to go into very much detail on that issue, partly because to do so would require examining a host of quite separate evidence and argument about how people learn, optimal class conditions, techniques of teaching and such like, which would be another book, and partly because, having some acquaintance with the relevant research, it is my view that there are many equally good ways of organizing and teaching such a curriculum.[3] The important points to make here are that the theoretical account of distinguishable components that need to be recognized as such by students does not necessarily mean that the elements have to be taught as separate elements or subjects rather than, for instance, integrated; nor that seeing the similarities and links between subjects is not equally important; nor that the elements have to be taught in an old-fashioned way, or indeed in any particular way. So let us, from this point on, simply ignore the irrelevant and misplaced jibe that the argument is designed to support a traditional view of schooling, and the false assumption that it leads necessarily to a curriculum organized in terms of subjects and a teaching approach that is long on passive imbibement of information and short on active learning. The argument has no such implications.

Notes and references

1. Who are 'they'? I am not referring here to scholarly papers, but to a popular, if confused, view that can be encountered amongst students, teachers, and ministry officials. If my experience is atypical, it will still be important to deal with this kind of argument, which has been recognized since the time of Plato, and may at any time become popular again.
2. See Salisbury, H., (1992), *The New Emperors; Mao and Deng,* London: Harper Collins.
3. For the other book that presents an argument for this view, see Barrow, R., (1984), *Giving Teaching Back to Teachers,* Brighton, Sussex: Wheatsheaf.

7. The Traditions of Thought and Inquiry

Literature

The argument implies that the goal of the educational process should be the development of individuals who can recognize logical distinctions, who can deal with different kinds of question in the appropriate manner, and who are imbued with the kind of understanding that history, literature, art, religion, ethics, science, mathematics, and philosophy can variously provide. In turn, it means that throughout the school years our teaching must be continuously concerned with language, seeking to increase vocabulary, to cultivate precision in its use, to enlarge understanding of the different ways in which it can be used to achieve different kinds of purpose, and, conversely, to enable the individual to understand and feel at ease with the subtle use of language by others, whether written or spoken. It means in addition that, however the curriculum is formally organized, the student needs to emerge with a grasp of the distinctive languages of science, philosophy, mathematics, religion, art, morality, history, and literature. In the case of science, for example, this implies an emphasis on understanding the concepts and nature of science, rather than simply on memorizing formulae or rote learning theorems and findings. (Whether it means concentrating on the written word or laboratory experience to a greater or lesser extent is an entirely different question. To which question, incidentally, the answer is surely that a balance is required. There may be evidence to support the view that hands-on learning experience is valuable in leading students to greater retentiveness, and possibly to a more thorough understanding. But the evidence does not establish that there is any necessary or inherent objection to book learning. One is tempted to conclude that variety is actually what matters.)

One is hard pressed sometimes in this business to know with whom one is arguing and whether or not one is tilting at windmills. My experience suggests that few teachers or parents would dissent from the mild comments I have so far made. On the other hand, we know that many educational theorists, and not a few official guidelines from ministries of education and the like, explicitly talk of the importance of seemingly quite other things such as self-expression, self-esteem, creativity, brainstorming, and communication, and make no reference at all to the things I have mentioned. We know also, though this may have nothing to do with what people intended, that many students leave school having a very poor command of language in the sense described above. And we know, more specifically, that in various jurisdictions history, literature, art, and philosophy in particular are not pursued in any systematic and serious way, while the curriculum does include such subjects as civics, social studies, creative writing, foreign languages and, wonder of wonders, job training. We know that even when command of language (sometimes misleadingly referred to as 'language skills') is formally valued, it can often be accompanied by an unwillingness to take active steps to develop it, on the grounds that such things as correction, damaging self-esteem, and interrupting spontaneity are to be avoided, and that students will come to develop the required understanding when they are ready to.[1] We know that there is resistance in some quarters to the idea of imposing what is seen as a middle-class, white, Western language on students, and we know that increasing agitation for 'political correctness' sometimes leads to greater concern for politically correct language than for command of language as such.

The above tendencies do not necessarily contradict the requirements of the argument. But, particularly in their cumulative effect, they produce a very contrary emphasis. The common feature of the random list of concepts mentioned above is that, in one way or another, they all presuppose understanding, if they are to be worthy of respect. There is no great merit in the self-expression of the ignorant, no value in the self-esteem of the foolish. Brainstorming amongst those who have no grasp or understanding of what they are brainstorming about is a sorry spectacle. One cannot be truly creative or imaginative if one does not proceed with understanding, since a creative work or an imaginative solution has to meet criteria of quality to count, and to meet such criteria one has to understand them. It is not, therefore, that I seek to repudiate the value of such things. Self-expression and self-esteem are certainly important, both in themselves and as means for encouraging the educational process: those who lack self-esteem or who are forbidden to express themselves are not likely to progress. But they lose their value when they are divorced from any standards. They need to be encouraged and developed within the context of understanding.

Similarly there is nothing necessarily wrong with social studies; using social studies as an umbrella might be (and often is) a good way of organizing the curriculum to cover such things as the development of historical understanding, philosophical finesse, and access to the arts and religion. But social studies is only educationally valuable so long as it *does* serve some such purpose. If it were to remain on the level of imbibing information about civic arrangements, then, while it would have a certain utility, it would be as a contribution to information gathering rather than education.

More generally, the question about such subjects as civics and social studies is whether they are being used as vehicles for developing aspects of the required understanding, as opposed to being brought forward as ways to replace that goal. The latter is certainly the implication of much contemporary rhetoric, which stresses the alleged 'relevance', 'appeal', and 'practical value' of various curriculum proposals rather than the value of the understanding they involve. But one cannot coherently justify curriculum proposals on such grounds as these. The issue is not whether the curriculum has instant appeal to students, is thought by them to be relevant, or indeed whether it does have relevance in the sense of immediate practical pay-off. The issue is whether it is relevant to, and instrumental in, developing the understanding that is our objective.

To be able to write creatively is no doubt most admirable. But the purpose of schooling is to allow all to understand and appreciate such things as the art of poetry rather than to produce poets. After all, the value of a poet, like anything else, goes down, the more commonplace the art.[2] Certainly, we also want there to be poets and, very likely, while some poets are so because of a visitation from the muse, others become so thanks to their school studies. None the less, the primary objective of the school is to develop understanding of creative poetry, just as it is to develop understanding of creative philosophy and creative science. Shakespeare's creativity does not primarily consist in tricks of the trade any more than does Einstein's. The basis of their achievement, in either case, is understanding. Producing creative writing, in other words, is not a necessary objective of the school, in the way that appreciating it is. In the second place, in order to appreciate it (and ultimately to produce it) one needs to develop the understanding built up over the centuries, rather than to study alleged techniques of writing creatively.[3]

Foreign languages often have an aura of mystery about them, and for a long time, regardless of the coming and going of educational fads, the ability to speak one or more foreign languages has been taken as a sign of intelligence.[4] ('Oh, he speaks three foreign languages, you know.') Why this should be so is a real mystery, given that all manner of people, including plenty of fools and knaves, can do so. Perhaps it is no more than a hangover from the days when it was as a matter of fact a mark of the educated person (i.e., of those who had received a formal schooling). At any rate, although languages may be very complex and hard to understand in a linguistic sense, there is no reason to suppose that learning to speak a foreign language is inherently difficult, and even less to suppose that doing so involves the intellect in any remarkable way. Any inherent

value to be found in studying a foreign language must surely reside in the fact
that it may involve the study of language *per se* (by way of the particular
species), or as a means to acquiring greater understanding of a particular
culture. (Quite different, of course, is the straightforward political and non-
educational argument, such as would be appropriate in Canada, that sometimes a
second language is needed to communicate with other members of society or that
considerations of respect and justice may demand official recognition of various
languages).

The above subjects, though they sometimes lack a clear educational
justification, might none the less be justified as part of the school's wider task.
But job training and other forms of activity that are directly geared to
employment arguably have no place in the school system at all. The fact that
they are increasingly to be found there is a symptom of the way in which the
school curriculum is increasingly designed by politicians rather than
educationalists. One key argument for a common schooling for all is precisely
to rescue individuals not only from ignorance and lack of personal development,
but also from a social situation in which they are moved into social positions
(i.e., jobs) by the luck of their birth rather than the development of their talents.
The more we move training schemes back into the school, the more we renege
upon that ideal. It is the job of industry to train its employees, not the job of the
schools. Their job is to develop such understanding as they can in individuals to
allow them to make their own informed, autonomous, decisions about what they
want to do, as well as to put them in a position to choose widely.[5]

Arguments have been produced for such claims as that one should not use the
word 'he' generically, that certain kinds of remark are sexist, racist, ageist, or
whatever, and that certain topics should not be discussed, certain claims not
referred to, certain books not read.[6] It would be rash to assert that any of these
arguments have been conclusive in terms of logic, though they have had
considerable impact sociologically. But the main question is not whether we
think particular points have been well or badly made, but whether we can accept
legislation on language from lobbyists. The fundamental issue that needs to be
thought and fought out here is the general one of freedom of speech, for, as John
Stuart Mill remarked with his customary lucidity, 'Strange it is, that men should
admit the validity of the arguments for free discussion, but object to their being
"pushed to an extreme"; not seeing that unless the reasons are good for an
extreme case, they are not good for any case'.[7] Everybody is in favour of
freedom of speech, except in certain cases where they don't like what they hear.
The question is whether there should be freedom of speech even when some
people don't like what they hear. Some, such as Mill, would argue for absolute
freedom of speech, but it is not necessary to take that position in order to argue

for the inappropriateness of importing notions of, for example, politically correct use of language into the school context: the school has no more right to tell people how to speak on contested ideological grounds than it has to tell them how to think. Its task in the latter case is to give them a wide understanding of how society has historically, and does now, think; it is not to make them share Galileo's views or the views of the church which tried to silence him, but to give them understanding of the position and arguments of both. In the same way (the more so because of the relationship between language and thought), it is anti-educational and therefore quite unacceptable to impose on students the requirement that they speak in a particular ideologically approved way. Correctness in language use does indeed matter, but it is correctness in terms of linguistic convention that we seek to impart - by definition, a wider view that already prevails, rather than a minority view that some wish to impose - rather than a substantive set of beliefs. Similarly, one can only sadly reflect that both logically and psychologically the rewriting of Agatha Christie, Enid Blyton and the like to remove unfashionable vocabulary and images, may lead to the rewriting of history, and finally to the burning of books. That is the point of Mill's argument.

Our objective in terms of language use should be to develop precision in respect of vocabulary and syntax in accordance with correct usage (i.e., the current convention amongst those who have an extensive command of language in relation to developed traditions of thought); but also, and perhaps more importantly, to develop linguistic power: that is to say, one teaches so as to enable people to understand, and themselves articulate, chains of reasoning that involve fine discrimination and careful and cogent argument. This leads to concern at a multiplicity of levels: one cares that students should appreciate the distinction between *'criterion'* and *'criteria'*, because precision is to be valued for its own sake and because of the understanding that such a distinction may betoken. One cares about the distinction between 'e.g.' and 'i.e.', because communication is confused if the two are muddled, and it is important to understand and be conscious of the difference between providing an example and giving the instance in question. One cares about the misuse of 'refute' to mean 'repudiate', because it obliterates the distinction between objecting to and producing solid grounds for objecting to something. On the other hand, one probably doesn't much care about the rival merits of 'different from', 'different to' and 'different than', because nothing hangs on the difference here in terms of sense, communication, or clarity of thought. One should care about the fact that the ubiquitous form 'type of persons' ('sort of things', 'kind of arguments') is incorrect, because it is a matter of logic rather than style that the phrasing should be 'types of person' ('sorts of thing', 'kinds of argument'). To use 'infer' and 'imply' as synonyms is not just to show ignorance of one's language; it is to lose one means of making a potentially necessary distinction, and more certainly it is to be unable to understand others who do have a grasp of the language, and thus in turn it leads to lack of communication. On the other hand, to use the generic 'he' in most contexts is not going to lead to any misunderstanding and does not betoken any failure to make distinctions: it is at worst a convention that may have had its day.[8]

This is not the place to continue listing examples, still less to attempt an exhaustive discussion. Suffice it to say that it is an important part of education to provide the kind of understanding of language that is contained within, say, Gowers' *Plain Words* or Partridge's *Usage and Abusage*.[9] From the beginning, then, schools need to have an active concern for the *minutiae* of language, and, as students begin to study particular issues and subjects, this concern must metamorphose into a like concern for precision and fine discrimination in physics, history, or for that matter stamp-collecting or discussion of pop music. But what else is important? What, besides exhibiting a general concern for language, do schools need to do? How, beyond this, does one develop the intelligence?

First and foremost by cultivating the study of literature. Such a claim immediately faces a double jeopardy, for, on the one hand, it seems so obvious to some that it is hardly worth stating, while, on the other hand, there are those who find it utterly bewildering and wonder why on earth the study of literature should be presumed to be any more likely to develop intelligence than the study of physics, politics, or snooker. It is therefore necessary to examine and explain this contention more fully.

First a word needs to be said about the manner of argument. One of the unfortunate consequences of the widespread inability to recognize logically distinct kinds of question for what they are is that the scientific paradigm has assumed a disproportionate and unjustified hold on our attention. By and large, people are aware of, and respectful of, the kind of argument that proceeds by the careful and systematic gathering of observable evidence, and that, through controlled experiment, establishes that such and such is the case. If the experts conduct a variety of experiments with nicotine and show that it is closely linked with cancer, people generally accept the conclusion that there is a causal relationship. Even those who preach an extreme version of subjectivism tend in practice to take note of this kind of research. They may say everything is a matter of opinion, but they none the less try to stop smoking.

Now, although the business of science and scientific inquiry rightfully commands our respect, there are two very serious dangers here. The first is that of taking an uncritical stance towards the various scientifically researched claims that are made, and the second is that of assuming that the scientifically demonstrated is the only kind of truth that we can put our trust in. In fact, of course, the employment of scientific procedures is no guarantee at all of a reasonable conclusion, even in relation to scientific questions. For the conclusion to be reasonable, the scientific procedures must have been both well conducted and appropriate. To examine whether these conditions are met takes us far beyond science as such. Rather more importantly, by its nature, science cannot directly substantiate the causal claims that are of so much importance to us, such as that smoking causes cancer. Even if the research is perfectly conducted, we are still left only with correlations or relationships between, in this case, smoking and cancer, and it is a matter of inference rather than demonstrated fact that the one causes the other. It is possible, as some have argued, that what actually causes cancer is anxiety, and that it is only because anxious people tend to smoke that smoking and cancer are so often found together. If experimentation is extensive and tightly controlled, the inferences that we draw may be said to be well founded and our conclusions, if not actually demonstrated, none the less entirely reasonable. None the less, there is a danger of placing too much trust in a claim simply because it is made following a process of empirical inquiry.

The second danger is much more important. Because, even if we are sometimes too trusting of scientifically derived claims, we are none the less right to respect this mode of inquiry, and because, broadly speaking, we understand it and see it to be a rational business, many people see the scientific mode of proof as the paradigm or only type of proof. Proof is thus equated with undeniable or uncontentious empirical demonstration. At its most extreme this view becomes an assumption that the only kind of truth we have any reason to believe in is that which has been proven in this sense of empirically demonstrated in an uncontentious manner. But there is no justification for this view at all: many truths, such as the truths of logic and mathematics, are in no way empirically demonstrable, but they are none the less true for that, and they can be shown (or demonstrated in a different sense) to be true by reasoning. Many other empirical claims may be true, and may be reasonably established as true, without it being possible to empirically demonstrate their truth. For example, it is true that I am now writing this sentence, it is true that it rained yesterday, it is true that there was a plot to assassinate Hitler in July, 1944. All of these are empirical claims, yet none of them can be incontestably established by experimentation. But that is no reason for us to regard them as any less reasonable claims than the claim that smoking causes cancer. (In addition there are numerous truths that are demonstrable but are not empirical, such as the truths of logic.)

The importance of this for our present purposes is that we must recognize that, while the claim that the study of literature is important for the development of intelligence cannot be experimentally demonstrated, that does not make it any the less secure as a claim. Furthermore, the requirement that an argument be entirely incontrovertible before we accept it is far too stringent. We have to make decisions and act in various ways throughout our lives. We cannot coherently take the view that where a proof is not uncontentious we have no reason to act in a certain way. As we have already seen, that approach would mean that we have no reason even to accept a number of experimentally supported claims - it is not, for example, incontestably demonstrated that smoking causes cancer. But in any case, the decision not to run across roads without looking, not to say something that might cause offence to a friend, to take daily exercise, to marry this person rather than that, to enter into a free trade agreement with another country - all such decisions have to be made, and we make them in the light of what it seems reasonable to conclude. We do not, and we cannot sensibly, expect or wait for unequivocal proof of any kind. And, finally, it should be noted that many decisions are necessarily and entirely reasonably based quite consciously on no assumptions about necessary consequences, but rather upon assumptions about likely or probable consequences. Not only is it not unequivocally experimentally demonstrated that drinking and driving is dangerous, it is not even necessarily true. But careful reasoning in the light of the evidence fairly obviously yields the conclusion that it is foolish to drink and drive. In other words, to justify an act or a policy, we do not have to have, and often cannot have, more than reason to think it likely that in general such and such will be the consequence of the action.

I do not claim, then, to be able to prove that the study of literature develops intelligence, in the scientific sense of proof. I do not claim that it is incontestable. I do not even claim that it necessarily will. The claim is rather that there is good reason, derived more from an understanding of what is involved in the concepts of intelligence and studying literature than from any empirically established correlation, to suppose that in general it is likely to contribute to the development of intelligence. And proof of this sort is quite sufficient to yield the conclusion that, if we care about intelligence, we ought to promote the study of literature.

As indicated in the previous paragraph, the essence of the argument lies in showing that there is a logical connection between the study of literature and some aspect or aspects of intelligence. It is therefore necessary to indicate what is meant by the study of literature. Given the recent proliferation of theories about what it means, or what it ought to mean, it is probably equally important to say what it does not mean. But since it would take a great deal of time to spell out all the particular views that I do not happen to share, I will content myself with stressing that I do not mean the study of literary theory on the one hand, nor, on the other, am I thinking in terms of a superficial imbibement of the surface content of literature. In other words, I am emphasizing both the word 'study' and the word 'literature'; while there may be much of interest to be said about how literature works, sociological interpretations of the art, and why it is important, the overall argument here is that it is the literature itself that should be the focus of the student's attention, and not theories about how to read it, how it came to be written, or why it is worth reading. Such questions are bound to be considered in the classroom from time to time, because they are important and interesting, and ultimately linked up to the way in which we read the material itself, but they are not a defining characteristic of studying literature: it is the literature, the work of the likes of Thomas Hardy and Scott Fitzgerald, we are studying, not the work of the likes of Northrop Frye, Jacques Derrida, or F.R. Leavis. (The university student may well have different priorities; my concern here is with a universal school education.) But I am also trying to convey by the word 'study' a closer relationship with the text than might be necessary to allow a student to answer comprehension questions of the type, 'what was the name of Pip's father?'. Just as a good teacher is very likely to discuss aspects of literary theory, so any intelligent reading presupposes knowing the answer to such questions (at least at the time of reading), but knowing such answers is by no means enough.

What is of central concern is getting students to read with enthusiasm and fluency books that they might otherwise find abstruse, unfamiliar, alien, or, more generally, difficult. Why is this valuable? Because books contain insights, ideas, arguments, characterizations, descriptions, and suggestions that are of good quality.

In essence the argument is as simple as that. To develop the intelligence is to develop the understanding of various logically distinct types of reasoning and various important subject matters. One does that by engaging the individual with such understanding. It is a contingent fact that the best of it is most conveniently accessible through books. One studies literature not to become a professional literary theorist, not to become expert in the novels of Jane Austen, or the style of Henry James, or the theme of nature. One studies it to engage with the content. Obviously, in order to achieve this end the teacher has to adopt some strategies and gradually instruct in various techniques. And so we start by instructing children how to form and recognize letters, we utilize comprehension exercises, we draw attention to style, we organize our reading around a theme, we talk about theories of literature. But all of these are merely means to the end, which is familiarity and ease with literature so that we can engage with the wisdom contained therein.

More could be said, particularly about various genres of literature. Reading poetry is different from reading fiction, and biography and *belles lettres* are different again. We could add points such as that fiction tends to focus on interpersonal relations or that poetry is crucially dependent on form. We could say that imagination is fed by literature. But, whatever we say, the key point remains that to be able to read Euripides, Shakespeare, Racine, Goethe, William Trevor, and Anthony Trollope is to be able to engage with sophisticated exploration of the human condition. A good teacher knows that there are better teachers than himself and wisely makes use of them.

Let me take one example. Anthony Trollope wrote a little-known novel called the *Fixed Period*. Written in 1880, it is set in 1980, which allows the author to make some potentially amusing predictions (in some cases accurate, in others not). Cricket, for instance, in Trollope's vision has become a game played between teams of 15 players using steam-powered machines for bowling. Such details, however, have little significance beyond their amusement value and possibly their power to set the reader thinking in a general way about the future and the business of predicting it. The essence of the book lies, first, in the usual Trollopian ironic and subtle treatment of human beings interacting, with their jealousies, pride, loves, and so forth, and secondly, more particularly, in the plot. The plot or story line revolves around the fact that in this futuristic state compulsory euthanasia is practised at the age of 67. At that age all citizens are removed, with much pomp and ceremony, to a college where they spend the final year of their life as a guest of the state, prior to having their veins opened and their bodies cremated. Despite the macabre theme, the book is very light-hearted in tone, and the major plot device is that the first person due to enter the college (an old friend of the President who tells the story and who created the euthanasia law), despite having been a staunch supporter of the proposal, is not surprisingly having second thoughts now that his time has come.

The traditional concerns of literary study are still important: how Trollope writes it is of considerable interest, and affects the nature of the story he tells. Theories about how we should read the text may have some bearing, some effect, on how we actually do. But the value of the work, from the point of view of the argument I am advancing, is as a particular kind of contribution to the subject of euthanasia and, more generally, as a contribution to the study of human beings in a social context. The novelist brings together the disciplines or developed traditions of thought that we have been at such pains to disentangle theoretically. In so doing he runs the risk of being at best less than fully on top of some aspect of the business, at worst of being thoroughly mistaken; but he gains the advantage of being able to consider the issue from a variety of angles and as it actually presents itself in life. This novel, for example, does not offer a full historical understanding of changing attitudes to euthanasia; it is not a careful treatise on religious values; it is not a philosophical examination of the topic in an academic sense: it does not, that is to say, define the term and marshall the purely rational arguments *in extenso*. Arguments are there, traces of the philosophical, glimpses of the religious, reference to the historical. But the distinctive feature, given that it is a novel, is that these elements and others are interwoven as they are in reality. Bits of the argument are there, but so are insights into how people might react to, utilize, or feel about such arguments. We are brought face to face with consideration of the topic in the context of human beings as human beings. It is a part of the debate no one can afford to miss.[10]

In short, while the values traditionally ascribed to the study of literature are not necessarily in dispute, and while the techniques of study enshrined in our academic traditions are not necessarily to be devalued, the real reason for caring about literature in the context of education is that it is the repository of human wisdom on matters that do not lend themselves to experimental resolution, analytic scrutiny, computation, and the like. It is a contingent point that, by and large, people who cannot and do not read, cannot exhibit much understanding. And it is not a necessary truth that those who are made to study literature will find their minds formed by it. But it is indisputable that if you want people to display the sort of understanding that literature enshrines, it is sensible to introduce them to it.[11]

It will be noted that I have ignored the question of which books should be read. And it is a question that by and large should be ignored - a red herring drawn across the main line of argument. The extreme view that no book is better than another is absurd. In this case we have criteria to judge by: we are talking about books that illuminate the human condition, and, on that score, some, such as Shakespeare, are clearly superior to others, such as Barbara Cartland. But really there is no need to get involved in such disputes. As far as they go, it is worth reading Cartland, Christie, and Rex Stout. But we need to go further. As to the Shakespeare versus Shaw argument, it need not be resolved. Read both, read either. The message is: enable students to read anything, then let them choose. The mistake has been to confuse 'being able to read anything', which requires that one be able to read what is initially difficult and alien, with 'being able to read *something*', which is altogether different and hardly an ideal to be proud of.

Traditions of Thought

The need to study the natural sciences and mathematics will scarcely be disputed and requires only a brief discussion, since we are not here exploring their nature, only whether there is some straightforward reason for valuing them educationally as they are conventionally conceived. The manner in which they should be studied is determined, as in all cases, primarily by an appreciation of the object of the exercise. The idea is not that every individual should become a competent scientist and mathematician of a high order, but that they should understand the nature of these activities, how they proceed, and why they proceed as they do. The more understanding that can be acquired of the natural world the better, because such understanding constitutes data that will be of importance in relation to intelligent decision-making in respect of all manner of problems, but the vital consideration is that the individual shall not simply memorize formulae, rote learn findings, and repeat experiments in the laboratory, but shall develop an understanding of why a certain kind of procedure is appropriate to a certain kind of question, should appreciate the difficulties and limitations in that procedure even in its proper place, and should recognize its inappropriateness to other kinds of problem. This rationale for studying science makes it largely immaterial whether the student concentrates on physics, chemistry, or biology. But since, as has been said, the content of science also has some importance, there is a *prima facie* case for favouring a general course in science that covers the broad domain of the natural sciences.

The problem with mathematics is in determining how far one needs to go. The need to be able to count, add, subtract, multiply, divide, and understand basic geometry and algebra is not likely to be questioned. Such understanding is necessary to intelligent performance in even the most humdrum of lives. Whether the individual actually needs to become immersed in calculus, trigonometry and the like (from the point of view of general intelligence rather than specialist needs) is debatable. I would hazard the opinion that he does not, either from the point of view of practical utility or our current concern with intelligence. Since I do not intend to pursue this question here, it will suffice to point out that the question is whether a lack of understanding of, say, trigonometry is likely to affect one's capacity to proceed through life in a manner that we would be prepared to call intelligent, in the way that lack of understanding the basic idea of number, shape and space, or of scientific method or historical perspective, clearly is.

Philosophical understanding is not necessarily best developed by the study of academic philosophy. What is meant here, it will be recalled, is developing an eye for conceptual questions and other logical problems, an understanding of how conceptual questions are to be treated, and an appreciation of the rules of logical reasoning. But here is a clear instance where emphasis on the need to develop this distinctive understanding does not necessarily lead to an argument for teaching it as a distinct subject.[12] If science, mathematics, history, art and religion are taught in the manner in which they need to be taught in order to develop intelligence, then philosophical understanding will necessarily be developed in these other contexts. To question the procedures of science, to consider why they are deserving of respect and what their limitations are, is to engage in philosophy. To study literature and question the legitimacy of euthanasia, or to wonder whether Emma is marrying for love, which raises in the mind the question of what love is, is to engage in philosophy. It is true that conceptual analysis is an activity that has particular rules, and it may be that a more direct consideration is required than would be afforded by untutored reflection on whether Emma is really in love. But then the spheres of art and history in particular afford an excellent opportunity for explicit examination of concepts (such as beauty, motive, and intention) in the philosophical manner.

The object of studying art is to understand it. It is not directly to cultivate appreciation of art in the sense of enthusiasm for it, so much as appreciation in the sense of awareness of what is involved, although appreciation in the latter sense is a necessary condition of genuine appreciation in the former sense, and we may thus regard such enthusiasm as a possible additional reason for encouraging the study of art. As with the natural sciences, the question of which art form should be studied is largely immaterial, since the primary object is to develop understanding of the aesthetic dimension or the nature of art in general, rather than to produce musicians, painters, or sculptors. A person who lacks any such understanding and who, for example, can only conceive of a painting in terms of its economic value, its size, or its value as a reminder of some place or person, is obviously debarred from making intelligent contributions to any debate about art. But he is also logically incapable of dealing intelligently with any problem that involves an aesthetic dimension. (Should the state subsidize opera? Is this design for the new town hall the most acceptable?) What is required in the name of art education, if our intention is to cultivate intelligence, is an understanding of traditions and theories of art. It is important to stress the tradition aspect, because those who say that aesthetic criteria are partly culturally specific are correct. To understand art is not to come to grips with a given set of phenomena, as is to some extent the case with the natural sciences. It is to come to grips with something that, regardless of innate human proclivity, has been shaped and developed by man. To understand music is at least partly to understand a particular tradition of music, so that, for example, to fully understand Prokofiev, it is necessary to know something about Mahler, about Beethoven before him, and so on back to Bach.

This consideration leads some to argue that the curriculum should involve the study of various traditions, in particular the traditions associated with various ethnic minorities, rather than the dominant Western tradition. It is perfectly true that there is, say, an Eastern tradition of art, which is distinguishable from a Western tradition, and, so far as any argument here goes, there is no reason to regard one as inherently superior to the other. There is furthermore something to be said for the argument that one way to improve one's understanding of anything is to set it alongside something similar but distinct (indeed that is an argument I use in respect of the value of historical study): trying to establish the differences and similarities between blues and country-and-western music, for example, is one way of arriving at a better understanding of both. On the other hand, the argument that there are various traditions of art and that all are to be equally valued is not satisfactory as it stands, and does not in any case yield the conclusion that we ought to study them all.

The argument is not satisfactory, because the admission that there may be diverse forms of art or artistic traditions which may be of equal value does not lead to the conclusion that all necessarily *are* equally valuable. After all, there are, or have been, various theories of medicine, and some may be as good as others, but they are not necessarily so, and rational arguments might be produced for saying that Western medicine is superior to the medicine of Haitian witchdoctors. Similarly, it might be argued that some cultures have relatively impoverished standards of art, and one might say, for example, that country-and-western music is an inferior species of art to opera. But if we ignore that line of reasoning, and conclude that in fact we have no reason to regard one artistic tradition as superior to another, then the proper conclusion would surely be that there are no aesthetic grounds for worrying about which tradition or traditions we study. The argument would become one of practicability and social pressure. As to that, it seems entirely reasonable to extend our interest to certain other major traditions, but quite unwarranted to ignore the tradition that has historically, and currently still does, dominate our society.

Why should we concern ourselves with religion at all, given that the philosophers tell us that religious faith is just that (a matter of faith, grounded in no recognizable provable claims), given that only a minority now publicly affirms such faith, and given that there are many religions of quite different kinds subscribed to by different believers? We must remember that our concern is with intelligence, that intelligence involves understanding, and that what needs to be understood is whatever is significant for interpreting the world. The fact is that religious faith has been of enormous historical significance, that it is still of such profound significance as to set the world to war, that it still leads to profound and sometimes violent disagreements, as, for example, in the case of the rivalry between fundamentalists and evolutionists, and that, while no religion may be ultimately provable in any sense, the religious view involves a major, distinctive, way of looking at, interpreting, and understanding the world. Whether one believes in a God or not may have very little to do with one's intelligence, but ignorance of what is involved will assuredly diminish one's chances of intelligent response to many issues. Some kind of understanding of the nature of religion is an important part of the intelligent person's repertoire.

Here what is needed is a basic philosophical grasp of the nature of religious concepts and the problems inherent in claims to religious knowledge, and some grasp of the major world religions. For that is the kind of understanding that is necessary to an intelligent response to major questions about society and nations.

The study of history, meaning an appreciation of the methods and problems of the historian and some grasp of the development of world history, in particular the basis of Western civilization, is another crucial contribution to the development of intelligence.[13] Intelligent people do not simply solve local and immediate problems. They have a sense of the way the world is and the part mankind has played in it.

There is a certain irony in the fact that the superficially Marxist belief that all social phenomena are historically determined is still widely entertained by people who appear to have very little grasp of history, and who, more particularly, paradoxically fail to draw the conclusion that the systematic study of history would be no bad thing. History provides the other column to complement that of literature as the basic supports for the arch of human understanding. The possibly sad truth is that there is no science of man: psychology, sociology, economics, politics and the like obviously have their value as academic pursuits, but not even their most earnest devotees could convincingly claim that they are sciences in the conventional sense, or that we have any reason to suppose that in principle we might arrive at the definitive explanation of human conduct. To understand what it is to be human must once again be recognized as the province of the arts, particularly of history and literature. Since almost every concept, every problem, every event, has a historical aspect, any approximation to a full or adequate understanding of life presupposes a degree of historical awareness and understanding.

We see, then, that the curriculum needs to be built around the study of science, art, mathematics, history, religion, and literature. Philosophy as such does not need to be specified, since it is an integral part of the way in which the remaining subjects need to be taught. Beyond encouraging the philosophical, teaching needs to be focused on enabling students to understand the nature and limits of the various traditional bodies of thought, and, in the case of religion, history, and literature, on the content. I have emphasized that dealing with these elements as distinct subjects does not necessarily imply teaching them as such (for example, consider the case of philosophy). But it does seem worth remarking that 'integration', which happens to be a popular idea (again) currently, may well be an unhelpful term. Far better would be 'co-ordination'. For it is part of the objective of this curriculum that students should be able to see links as well as distinctions, and it is important that the end product should be a person who does not compartmentalize, but who can draw on any necessary part of his understanding at any time.

The stress that I have placed on content, particularly in the case of literature and history, may lead the unwary to associate this view with the Great Books approach to education, or Hirsch's more recent view of 'cultural literacy'.[14] There is no significant connection. The idea of basing a university education on certain selected Great Books is certainly not without merit, however unfashionable it may currently be, and is not incompatible with anything I have said. None the less, I am arguing for a great deal more than that, not only in the range of reading required, but in the systematic study of various disciplines. While many of Hirsch's criticisms of the current state of affairs in America are telling, his proposed solution, to base the curriculum on a vast check-list of reference points, seems to me ridiculous. It is true that a widespread ignorance of a large number of his reference points is revealing, especially if students are also ignorant of alternative reference points, as I am sure many are. But the reason that it matters if nobody knows who Churchill was, what the Declaration of Independence says, who wrote David Copperfield, etc., is that this betokens a failure to get to grips with history, with literature, and so on. The only sane solution is a curriculum grounded in significant traditions of thought. Only thus can we hope for an intelligent citizenry.[15]

Notes and references

1. Kieran Egan doubts that anyone would object to 'correction, damaging self-esteem, and interrupting spontaneity' absolutely, that they would more likely believe there to be times when they would be inappropriate and there to be various preferable strategies. Where has he been recently? In my experience there are plenty of people who both talk and act this way, but in any case my interest, as throughout this book, is in the argument about what position it is most reasonable to hold, rather than the empirical question of how many people do hold various positions.
2. Perhaps an historical argument could be set against this claim. Was poetry valued the less at those times and in those places where making verses was one of the expected accomplishments of the educated and civilized?
3. This is not to deny inspiration or to challenge, e.g., Coleridge. It is not denied that some individuals may have intuitive understanding.
4. Going back at least to the Romans, amongst whom the ability to speak Greek was one mark of the educated in late Republican times.

5. For further discussion of this topic, see Barrow, R., (1981), *The Philosophy of Schooling*, Brighton, Sussex: Wheatsheaf.
6. Some Canadian examples include a ban on the reading of *The Merchant of Venice* in a BC School district, the Philippe Rushton affair in Ontario, the Keegstra affair, the adoption of a non-sexist language policy by UBC Faculty of Education. For a more detailed discussion of this issue, see Barrow, R., 'Censorship and Schooling', in Spiecker, B. and Straughan, R. (eds), (1991), *Freedom and Indoctrination in Education*, London: Cassell. See also, DelFaltore, Joan, (1992), *What Johnny Shouldn't Read*, New Haven: Yale University Press, and Hentoff, N., (1992), *Free Speech for Me - But not for Thee*, London: Harper Collins.
7. Mill, J.S., (1910), *On Liberty*, Ch. 2, London: Dent.
8. See further on this topic, Barrow, R., (1982), *Injustice, Inequality and Ethics*, Brighton, Sussex: Wheatsheaf. It is important that we do not confuse teaching a given usage as correct with trying to change or arrest language on grounds of correctness. There may not be (is not, in my view) much of a case for ordering adult language users to mend their ways, or in trying to police them. But it is very different to explain and encourage current usage among those developing a language.
9. Richard W. Bailey has recently (*Images of English: a Cultural History of the Language*, Cambridge; Cambridge University Press, 1992) drawn our attention both to the very long history behind claims about the quality and value of English as a language and to the extent to which diametrically opposed claims have been, and still are, made. The overall direction of his argument is that claims about the superior quality of English as a language, and of so-called 'standard English' within the language, are unconvincing. His argument, however, does not affect my more limited contention that some subspecies of English may be relatively inadequate for the particular purpose of rational reflection on abstract matters. In any case, the issue (as it concerns me) is not the alleged superiority of English, or a particular form of it, but the importance of all individuals having access a) to a common language, and b) to a command of language sufficient in scope and style to the purpose of intellectual understanding. One point worth noting: Bailey at times fails to distinguish questions about dialect from questions about the scope of subspecies of a language. Most, if not all, of his examples involve claims about dialects. But the suggestion that Yorkshiremen cannot discuss existentialism because of their distinctive vocabulary, phrasing, and accent is ridiculous, in a way that the suggestion that the language of certain other identifiable groups may be inadequate for such a purpose is not.
10. Kieran Egan is aghast at my failure to recognize that literature is centrally to do with a transaction of emotion, infuriated by my reference to 'reality', and shocked by my refusal to engage with various theories and discussions of literary criticism. His reaction seems a trifle excessive. That literature is partly about the 'transaction of emotion' I do not dispute, though it is not a phrase I would have chosen; on reality, I have already said enough in the course of the book to make it clear that I accept neither the view that reality is altogether given, nor the view that we entirely create it. The fact that novelists contribute to forming our sense of reality is readily acknowledged. The suggestion that therefore one cannot talk of the novel as being (more or less) realistic is repudiated. Finally, I am not here interested in examining rival literary theories. I am expounding my own view that, whatever anyone else may care to say, there seems very good reason to emphasize the content of literature when considering its educational value, 'content' here referring primarily to the sum total of the characterization and action of the story.

    Novelists themselves, of course, know rather more about the matter than critics and theorists. From Jane Austen - 'only a novel . . . in short, only some work in which the most thorough knowledge of human nature, the happiest delineation of its varieties, the liveliest effusions of wit and humour are conveyed to the world in the best chosen language' (*Northanger Abbey*, 1818) - to D. H. Lawrence - 'And being a novelist, I consider myself superior to the saint, the scientist, the philosopher and the poet, who are all great masters of different bits of man alive, but never get the whole hog' ('why the novel matters', *Phoenix*, 1936) - by way of Henry James - 'But then I'm a battered old novelist and it's my business to comprehend' (letter to Edward March, 1915). As Richard Hughes urged, 'Do your bit to save humanity from lapsing back into barbarity by reading all the novels you can' (in a speech at Foyle's Literary Luncheon, 1975). But then again, 'Oh Ken, be careful, you know what he's like after a few novels' (Monty Python's Flying Circus, 1969)!
11. It will come as no surprise to the reader that I am more or less in full sympathy with John Carey's argument (*The Intellectuals and the Masses: Pride and Prejudice among the Literary Intelligentsia, 1880 - 1939*, London: Faber and Faber, 1992) that during the last hundred years intellectuals in the sphere of the arts seem almost wilfully to have become unintelligible (or at any rate totally

unconvincing), as if to distinguish themselves from the masses. (Though I am disappointed that he has chosen to cite George Gissing as an example.) To those who claim, therefore, that I am flying in the face of much recent critical theory, I say: a good thing too. Let's get back to reading literature, rather than theories about reading it, and let literature be both about human life and intelligible to the literate majority.

12. This is not to say that it would necessarily be undesirable to teach it as a distinct subject.

13. I hope I have said enough to indicate that I recognize the value of various other cultures, and that the school system certainly needs to have concern for developing understanding both of the fact of cultural diversity and of particular different cultures. None the less, for reasons that should be apparent in the main text, I have no hesitation in emphasizing the crucial importance in the Western world of providing understanding of the basis and nature of Western civilization.

14. Hirsch, E.D., (1987), *Cultural Literacy*, Boston: Houghton Mifflin.

15. I should comment on a currently favoured approach to curriculum which would build it around fashionable (usually 'socially aware') topics. Thus, out go old-fashioned studies in history, literature, or science, and in come feminist studies, environmental studies, Aids education, death education, and the like. In theory, this is not altogether a bad idea. It is logically possible to start with particular problems or areas of interest, and in the process of studying them to work outwards or backwards to the various elements they involve, and then to develop the understanding necessary to cope with the elements. From the organizational or teaching point of view, however, this is going to be a nightmare. All teachers would need to be equipped to deal with all aspects of a given topic. Well, perhaps that is not an unreasonable, even if it is a somewhat unrealistic, ideal. But then all students are either going to have to proceed at the same pace, or rapidly move off into studying at their own pace. The problem that started the process will in fact necessarily not be dealt with until years after its introduction.

8. Liberal Democracy, Liberal Education, and the Cultivation of Intelligence

The Idea of a Liberal Education

A great deal of scholarship takes the form of criticism of previous scholarship. This is scarcely surprising, since it is natural that we should modify and build on the work of our predecessors, or feel the need to reject their work altogether to make room for our own alternative views. Thus Aristotle modified, and in some respects rejected, Plato; Marx wanted to develop Hegel, some say turn him on his head; and in our own day many valuable works have taken as their starting point the criticism and rejection of other works. Understandable as it may be, the fairly constant knocking and discrediting of the arguments of others is a feature of scholarship that some find rather wearisome. Other features that may with reason cause some to feel impatient include: the narrowly specialized nature of much inquiry, which sometimes leads to a very partial if not misguided view of the matter in hand; the increasing tendency to dwell on metatheory, by which is meant speculative theorizing about the nature of theorizing, rather than with theorizing about something substantive (some would say *doing* something substantive); the academic imperatives, such as the need to secure funding and to write in certain ways and in certain kinds of journal to establish credibility; and the extensive lack of agreement amongst scholars in many critical areas. The outsider who has some familiarity with the scene might well be forgiven for seeing scholarship as a rather irritating game, that seems increasingly uninterested in establishing basically reasonable contentions about important matters, and that, in the event, serves more to indulge the participants' sense of importance than to reveal anything significant about ourselves and our world. To come to the matter in hand, for all the academic work in linguistics, psychology, sociology, and philosophy, can anybody in *academia* say something clear, educationally significant, and relatively uncontentious about intelligence, that could not have been said by a moderately well-educated and thoughtful bank-clerk?

117

If the answer to this question is far from certain, part of the reason lies in the awkward fact that judgements of value are ultimately crucial to answering most questions, including questions about means to ends, and questions of value are usually extremely difficult to resolve. If there is no science of determining where we ought to be going, as there certainly isn't, and no other agreed way of doing so, which is considerably less certain but is popularly supposed, then how on earth can we say anything sensible about how to get there?

At rock bottom, educational arguments are political: how we conceive education, how we ought to proceed in schools, what sort of a curriculum we should have, even what techniques of teaching to adopt, all presuppose a view of the kind of world we want, the kind of people we want to be - in short, our values. To some extent this otherwise obvious truth was obscured during the years in which educational theory was dominated by a scientific conception of psychology and an unselfcritical style of analytic philosophy.[1] In those days, the implicit assumption was that the ends would be determined through analysis by the philosopher-experts, and the means would be experimentally determined by the psychology-experts. In retrospect, it seems amazing that nobody noticed that the psychologists were by and large producing evidence about means to quite different ends from those generally advocated by the philosophers. But, in any case, these days there is a great deal of justified criticism of earlier psychological research on its own terms, and an equally justified rejection of the idea that philosophical expertise enables one to reveal the values or ends that we truly ought to hold. The perceived problem of the subjectivity of value judgements is back with us in a big way, at its most strident taking the form of asserting that one's values are merely a matter of personal taste, with the inevitable consequence that any practice or means might in principle be as good as any other.

But that is only 'in principle'. In principle a person might hold any value, but in fact people don't. Very few people would be prepared to say, surely very few believe, something such as that it is morally acceptable to torture one's political opponents in horrific ways or even to silence them; rather, people who in fact condone specific instances of such acts claim to share various values with us, but claim that the actions in question can be justified in the light of those values. Whether that turns out to be true or not, we have at least moved into a realm where rational discussion is possible. And such similarities of opinion as there are between us, and there will be some amongst almost all human beings, give us some kind of bedrock on which to base our reasoning. 'Look,' we say, 'you agree that x is important, and surely you see that that implies y, and if this evidence I have about z is correct, as surely we have reason a for believing it is, then doesn't it follow that given *b*, which implies *c*, which is logically related to *y*, *it doesn't make sense* for you to persist in saying that it is justifiable to do *m'*.[2]

One implication of the above is that in the end serious arguments about serious matters cannot take place within the boundaries of academic discourse as it is currently constituted. You cannot have a purely abstract argument about ends, or, therefore, about means that presuppose contestable ends. You have to have an argument with some particular person, or persons, and the participants have to be sincere in admitting what they do value. Thus, one does not prove or reasonably establish that intelligence of a certain sort is to be valued; one convinces particular people that on reflection they see value in such intelligence. One does not demonstrate; one convinces particular people. But one convinces, or attempts to, by a rational process rather than by the force of one's rhetoric or the strength of one's personality.

Another, subsidiary, implication is that one can only succeed if those with whom one is arguing are relatively intelligent people. This is the problem we face with fanatics of all types, and in the academic world, with people whose 'intelligence' is formed by adherence to some ideology rather than by a breadth of understanding. Trying to have a rational discussion about abortion with one whose position is based upon the idea of a woman's right to choose, yet who has no understanding of the long history of philosophical discussion of rights, and has never entertained ideas about the concept of a person, is going to be difficult. (I choose this example, incidentally, because I happen to share the conclusion. The issue is precisely *not* whether their view is right or wrong, but whether they are in a position to show by reason that, given some shared assumptions, it follows that one should hold this view.)[3]

In general terms, my strategy has been to make the necessary criticism of other views that are so different in kind as to need clearing away before we can proceed, and then to try and link my claims by a chain of reasoning to some starting points that are likely to be widely accepted (such as that it is better to understand than not to understand).[4]

A question worth raising at this juncture is: are things any better now, in respect of the education we provide, than they were, say, ninety years ago? The question is worth asking because they ought to be better, if all the research and theorizing we have engaged in had significance, yet I do not see any obvious reason for supposing that they are. Admittedly, this is not the kind of question that can be answered with much certainty, still less in some quantitative manner. The sorts of instrument that educationalists would typically want to make use of, such as literary tests, general knowledge quizzes, number of people who go on to university, number of 'A' levels or scores on other public examinations, all beg the question in one way or another. Certainly, we provide education to a higher level for more people than we did, but this, while it may be a good thing even if the education we provide is not particularly good, doesn't answer the question of whether the education that we do provide successfully is any better than it was in the past.   Whether people's literacy ratings, or general knowledge, or examination grades are better than their grandparents' were (assuming they received a 'good' education) begs the question of whether these are appropriate criteria for judging a well-educated person. Once again, we see that a necessary first step in any educational discussion is clarifying the concept of education so that we are clear about what counts as educational success. But my immediate point is that I see no obvious reason to assume that the successful school leaver of today - by which is meant the kind of student who is deemed to have done averagely well - is any better educated, in the sort of sense I have outlined, than the successful school leaver of the past. His scientific knowledge will be more up to date (and, in a way, greater), because the content of science is one thing that does change and in some sense increase. But there is no reason to suppose that his literary or historical knowledge will be any greater, no reason to suppose that his understanding will be any greater, and no reason to suppose that he will have a broader understanding.

Now, for all that I have said, there is no reason to suppose the opposite either. Since no reasons are being given, there is no reason to suppose anything. But, as I have said, there is something odd about this, because, if our ends have remained the same, all our industry in researching improved means might be expected to have paid off. Well, perhaps it has. But I doubt it, for this reason: the research into means has not been connected to the ends that we generally had in mind in the past, nor to the very different ends that some people have in mind now. Paradoxically perhaps, the empirical research into education over the last fifty or so years, the kind of research that is popularly supposed to be relatively practical and concrete, has been largely irrelevant to anyone's conception of education. Instead it has been conducted in the light of a conception that was expressly constructed to allow of empirical research. The real change has been in the area of conceptions of education. So the question of whether we are doing any better is really a question of whether we have a more convincing conception of education. And my answer to that is negative.

This book has been partly about the value of what is often called a liberal education. An education that is liberal both in that it is conceived in wide and generous terms, rather than confined to narrow specialism, and in that it liberates the individual from the deadly constraints of the here and now, the particular and the concrete. This was a conception that was to the fore at the turn of the century (notwithstanding the fact that it was generally supposed to be suited only to the few), that is still vigorously championed by some, but that is in practice losing ground daily. The evidence for that assertion can be found, though not systematically provided here, in what we do in schools, what theoreticians say about education, what governments mandate in education, and what society provides for so-called educated people in newspapers, political debate, mass-media, and bookstores. It seems quite reasonable to say that mass education has not produced a mass of liberally educated people. The reason being, primarily, that few people have been trying to produce them.

The liberally educated person has what I term 'the educated intelligence'. The 'educated intelligence' is defined in terms of a broad understanding that encompasses an awareness of logically distinct kinds of question and bodies of thought that between them encompass the most important dimensions of human ways of looking at the world and the most important contributions to understanding the world and what it is to be human. Such understanding forms the basis of our knowledge and our imaginative and creative abilities. In addition, the educated intelligence involves a concern for truth, reasonableness, precision, accuracy, clarity, open-mindedness, and tolerance.

As has been consistently acknowledged, one cannot prove that this constellation of attributes represents what intelligence means. But I have argued that it makes sense of what seems to be common ground in the way we think of intelligence, and that intelligence in this sense is to be valued. Its value likewise was not *proven*, but particular objections were dealt with, and the suggestion made that, once fully understood, it is difficult to imagine any of us (I cannot speak for Martians, or even classical Spartans, but I do aim to speak for any readers of this book, whatever their race, gender, citizenship, and so on) coherently denying its value without some kind of inconsistency. Nor can one prove that the sort of curriculum I then outlined, in particular its emphasis on literature, would develop such intelligence. It cannot be proved, because it is not necessarily the case: individuals could develop such intelligence on their own, and many will pursue such study without noticeable benefit. None the less, given what is meant by the educated intelligence and given what is involved in the curriculum, seeing the logical connections between them, we may reasonably conclude that it seems likely that in general such a curriculum will contribute to the goal.

As people never tire of pointing out, we live in a world of rapid change and awesome responsibility. This is part of the price we pay for living in an open society, which, by and large, we value. From time to time, certain dogmatists who feel that they know what is good for everyone, or frustrated individuals who feel they can no longer cope with the uncertainty, are tempted to espouse the idea of a closed society (though at this particular moment in history, with the collapse of the Soviet Union and the difficulties in the attempt to transform South

Africa, such an escape route is considerably less popular than it has been). And, despite recent events, it is arguable that closed societies can in some sense work: they are likely at any rate to provide a degree of stability for the average citizen, and they might succeed in promoting a sense of security and well-being. But our society is committed to certain values that are incompatible with such an option, in particular the values of the search for truth and individual autonomy, with the consequence that some form of democratic government, some kind of free and open society, is a given. In such a society, education has to be of a certain sort: it has to be directed at developing the understanding of individuals, at increasing their autonomy, and enabling them to cope with the responsibility of decision-making. Fukuyama has recently argued that liberal democracy is the end of a natural historical process; it is the ultimate form of government, that cannot and will not be improved upon.[5] This neo-Hegelian thesis (which would have amazed Hegel a great deal more than even the Marxist version of his view) strikes me as totally unconvincing and implausible. But, while there is no reason to assume that it is inconceivable that liberal democracy should be improved upon, it is the form of government that, of those we can currently envisage, we are determined to defend. And since there is no reason to accept the suggestion that it is the inevitable product of the evolution of history, there is every reason to be perpetually vigilant about its defence. In other words, I do not argue here for the value of liberal democracy, although such argument can be provided. Rather, I take it as a premiss, and observe that its successful continuation is dependent on a continued conscious effort to defend it and make it work, particularly through education.

Thus, the framework in which the particular argument of these pages has been set is the view that the idea of a liberal education has gradually been losing its appeal over the last hundred years, and that it is essential for the sake of the kind of society we value to reassert its crucial importance.

Educating for Intelligence

Questions to do with the elementary or primary school are of less concern to me than questions to do with the secondary school. This is not because I think them unimportant. The early years of schooling are obviously extremely important in influencing the likely shape of future developments in the individual. Furthermore, there are important questions to be asked about our practice at this level. Are we too much governed by a questionable model of psychological development? Are we too much inclined to assess primary teachers in terms of their personal qualities and their attitude to children, at the expense of their intellectual understanding? Is the elementary curriculum too much given over to integration and nurturing the self-confidence of the individual, at the expense of instilling standards and understanding? But, though these and other questions can reasonably be asked, our understanding of the goal of the early years of education is relatively clear and widely shared: however we think it should be organized, most of us believe that young children should be taught to read, write, and count - the necessary foundation skills for subsequent education - that a spirit of inquiry should be fostered, and that the child's confidence and enthusiasm should be developed.

The secondary school is the focus of my attention because it is at this level that we succeed or fail in turning the basic skills to good use and in providing an education, and it is at this level that real differences of opinion emerge, explicitly or implicitly, as to what we are trying to achieve - as to what should count as a successful education. My argument has been that essentially we should judge the quality of a school by the understanding that it develops in students: understanding of what has been, of what is, and of what might be. This understanding necessarily has to encompass, by some means or other, the scientific, the philosophical, the arts, religion, ethics, mathematics, literature, and history. If any one of these is ignored then we do not merely run the risk of leaving a gap in the individual's understanding, as those who happen to know nothing of the French revolution, the environment, or stamp-collecting, have a gap; much more seriously, we run the risk of distorting all of their understanding, for the person who lacks philosophical understanding cannot make coherent use of his scientific understanding, the person who lacks any historical awareness cannot fully understand religion, the person who has no inkling of religion cannot understand history, the person who lacks the insights provided in literature lacks insights that are relevant to all manner of ethical, philosophical, and artistic issues.

The secondary school curriculum should involve a systematic engagement with the best that has been thought and said. This is not primarily an aesthetic judgement. That is to say, the reference is not to the best works of art, but rather a reference to the most intelligent contributions made throughout history to the various types of understanding. The object should be to bring students to a point at which they can, with ease, pleasure, and engagement, read an Einstein, a Shakespeare, a Gibbon, a Plato, a St Augustine, a Gombrich, a Tolstoy, a Hawking, or a Russell.

Arguments about which works are the best, and, still more, arguments about whether and how one can determine which works are best, are obscuring the fact that to a marked extent our schools are not even trying to engage with the best. Their mission is being conceived in quite other terms, both by the presentation of theoretical alternatives and by our practice. Although inevitably I have to make reference to particular examples, and for simplicity and convenience I have used obvious and famous names, it is no part of my argument that students should necessarily study the work of the particular people mentioned. The argument is that they ought to be able to read authors of this calibre with enjoyment and understanding, rather than be doomed to remain on the level of the *Reader's Digest*, the *Sun* newspaper, Jeffrey Archer or *Seventy-two Ways to Take Yourself Too Seriously*. Nor is this a mindless élitism: in the first place, the claim is not that the *Reader's Digest,* or romances and detective stories, are necessarily shameful products without any value, but rather that by perfectly straightforward criteria they are inferior to some other works in certain specific respects: Anthony Trollope provides a more searching and subtle analysis of human character than Agatha Christie does (and that 'judgement', if such it be, is more nearly an indisputable fact than it is a subjective matter of opinion). His work is therefore more relevant to developing the kind of understanding we are concerned with. Secondly, if élitism comes into it, it would seem that it is those who on no real evidence persist in talking as if some people were by nature incapable of coming to grips with such thought who are the élitists. There is certainly nothing élitist in arguing that the best that has been thought and said, whatever it may be, should be made accessible to as many people as possible.

The teacher, at least according to the conception of education put forward here, is an individual whose primary task is to develop understanding. He or she is not a social worker, a facilitator in some unspecified sense, or a counsellor. There are of course questions to be raised about means, though they happen not to be the concern of this book, and it may be that the task of teaching will be easier and more effective if the individual has certain social interests and abilities. But the fact remains that the quality of a teacher is to be judged first and foremost by his or her ability to communicate understanding rather than by a capacity to interrelate in any other kind of way. The theories of such educationalists as Dewey, Montessori, and Neill owe more to a concern to motivate and interest the uninterested, than to a clear alternative conception of education. They have been misappropriated by some as novel theories of education rather than as (questionable) theories of teaching. As theories of motivation in exceptional cases they may have some merit. But as theories of motivation in general they are without plausibility, and the evidence is clear that children have been and can be motivated by a wide variety of techniques. The important point is that in advocating new techniques of teaching we should not throw out the baby (i.e., a worthwhile content) with the bath water (i.e., a particular technique).

The centrality of the question of content, then, the vital importance of basing all educational discussion on a clear view of what it is valuable to understand, has been emphasized. And it is important to do this, both because it is true and because it is unfashionable. It is true that in some places, such as England with its government-inspired common curriculum, attention is currently focused on content. However, in general, such a focus still does not find favour with educationalists (and it might be added that, though the common curriculum in England addresses the right issue, it does not do so in a particularly coherent way). But in emphasizing the importance of content when it comes to developing intelligence, we must avoid swinging to the other extreme, concentrating only on information, facts, and figures, and ignoring the question of how the content needs to be approached. Understanding has to be embedded in particular contexts, both because it is incoherent to imagine it divorced from a context, and because it takes different forms in different contexts. In addition the value of understanding varies from context to context. None the less, it must be stressed that it is *understanding* that we are concerned with, and not simply the ability to memorize, recite, parrot, and reproduce information, however sophisticated or useful. And since we are concerned to develop understanding, we are logically obliged to approach teaching in a certain kind of way. Hence, notions such as critical thinking, self-discovery, creativity, imagination, and inquiry, do have an important part to play in education. But they need to be interpreted in the context of specific bodies of thought. The idea that such things are generic skills is seriously misleading: one cannot meaningfully be said to have critical thinking skills or creative skills in the abstract, without qualification. One has to be thinking critically about something or being creative in some context, and the ability to do so in one sphere does not guarantee the ability to do so in another, because such ability presupposes understanding of a sphere. Thus the teacher has to develop a critical, inquiring, creative, imaginative approach to things that matter, such as history, science, and art.

Human beings are not machines. They are not simply programmed data collections as are computers. Though we have evidence that the human brain is to some degree mechanistic, and may conceivably be so to a greater degree than hitherto supposed, the fact remains that people have intentions, motives, fears, passions, likings, a sense of awe, insight, intuitions, and other such characteristics that cannot be satisfactorily explained in mechanistic terms.[6] More generally, human beings do not simply respond automatically to input, they do not merely calculate: they understand, and the concept of understanding implies a self-consciousness that is the hallmark of being human. A computer can produce the answer. Only a human being can *see* that it is the correct answer, because only a human being has awareness and understanding.

At any given time, a society will have its own particular priorities and list of topical issues - the skills of hunting and fishing, perhaps, and a decline in the buffalo population; at another time, the skills of the doctor and lawyer, and the needs of industry. At the present time, a great deal of attention is paid to the needs of the work-place and such issues as the environment, Aids, gender and racial equity, and social issues. But it is quite inappropriate to let even pressing current concerns drive a curriculum.[7] In the first place, the school is not designed to be a feeding system for the work-force. To treat it as such is likely to lead to a poor preparation for work, since, when all is said and done, banks know more about how to train people to work in banks, the police force about how to train police, industry about how to train assembly-line workers and managers, and so on, than schools do. It also leads to an outrageous limitation on the options available to individuals. The school's purpose is, on the contrary, by providing an education, to open up possibilities to the individual. In the second place, there is no value in discussing topical issues *per se*; the value lies in discussing them intelligently, and that requires understanding of the various types we have considered. The school's task is not to solve the problems, but to provide the understanding that ultimately enables citizens to discuss social issues intelligently.

If we think of the kinds of event that actually, historically, have shattering impact on mankind, we see that they are for the most part the product of the uncritical acceptance of systems of thought. Misguided Marxism was a far more serious issue than Aids is likely to be. (At a conservative estimate, 150 million dead, often hideously tortured, and who knows how many others who suffered but survived, under Stalin and Mao. But the quantity and the nature of the horror are perhaps less to the point than the fact that, unlike Aids, humans 'wished' this evil upon humanity. It need never have happened.) Nazi doctrine caused a great deal more suffering than cigarettes or over-logging are likely to do. Religious intolerance and Fascism have led, and still do lead, to far more destruction and misery than women as a group have ever had to face. This is not to deny the importance of issues such as Aids or even smoking, but it is to insist on the enormous importance of equipping people to make autonomous assessments of systems of thought, and to ask why there are school leavers who know more about the dangers of smoking than the dangers of totalitarianism. Besides, the only way that society is ever going to be able to come up with a solution to the problems of the environment, sexually transmitted diseases, and social issues, is through a combination of scientific and philosophical understanding. In the meantime, what can we do to guard against the likelihood of future ideological horrors? No skill-training programme is going to have any relevance to the issue, no attempt to foster alleged generic mental abilities of critical thinking or imagination is going to prove effective. Only by developing in individuals a thorough understanding of the past, by expanding their understanding of what it is to be human, by developing philosophical understanding, by providing insight into religion, and so on can we hope to avoid such things in the future.[8]

The intellectual capacity is enhanced and developed by exercise. But the exercise has to be in the context of logically distinct kinds of reasoning and important and substantial bodies of thought. Such bodies of thought also nurture the creative and imaginative capacity. What better way to stimulate the mind to an awareness of the possible implications of the drive to so-called 'political correctness', than to study the Bolshevik revolution or to read Orwell's *1984*? How are people who have no understanding of the nature of religious belief in general, or of various religions in particular, supposed to form reasonable views about religious tensions in a society? To hear some people's objections to emphasizing Western culture, one would imagine that they were quite ignorant of the fact that, say, Islamic culture is an historical outgrowth of the Hellenistic and Roman Empires, i.e., of the world of Western culture. Understanding the past and the foreign is essential to understanding the present, and, one might add, generally extremely appealing to the young, despite contemporary educationalists' curious fixation with confining them to the study of the here and now.

Something like a Hegelian synthesis is needed to consolidate this next great leap forward in education, (which is, of course, also a step backwards, to regain something of value that we have lost). Historically, the idea of filling the empty vessel of the mind with the received wisdom of the world was countered by the idea of the individual discovering knowledge for himself. But so long as this voyage of discovery was conceived of as being a process, with no particular content, it was at least as risible as what it was intended to replace. We now see the need to harness the active journey of the mind to a specific kind of content.

Reaching back into the past in this way is nothing to be ashamed of. Certain branches of knowledge, particularly the empirical, do progress in a fairly straightforward way.[9] Our knowledge of the natural sciences and medicine is considerably greater than that of our forebears. Though even here the notion that we have got it all wrapped up is scarcely tenable, one would hardly recommend reading even the classic medical treatises of the past, except as part of a lesson in appreciating how wide of the mark what is taken to be fact at any time may be. But in areas such as the arts, history, literature, philosophy, and religion - in other words the bulk of the content we are concerned with - there is by no means necessarily a steady line of progress. Techniques of various sorts, specific skills, and specific operations may improve steadily, and what is done and believed today has to some extent arisen out of the beliefs and actions of the past. But the fact remains that the contribution to philosophy of an Aristotle, though one may say that in some ways it is dated, can still be as important and relevant to debate today as any contemporary work, and there would be nothing odd about judging it to be superior in quality. Likewise, one may quite coherently argue for the superior quality of Greek architecture over modern architecture, the superior religious insights of Thomas Aquinas over the current Archbishop of Canterbury, the superior quality of Bernard Shaw over John Osborne, and so forth. The cult of the contemporary, which is a feature of our schools, is another tendency that militates directly against our chances of developing the intellect. However, recognizing the importance of the past, both as a subject for study and as a repository of works of quality, does not mean deriding the present, nor does it imply any desire to arrest development. One can value the nineteenth-century style of fiction and at the same time welcome twentieth-century developments. Conversely, one can believe that contemporary historians have improved on Gibbon in various respects, but none the less recognize that Gibbon is worth reading.

The fundamental point is that our sense of reality is structured partly by what is out there in the world and partly by what we bring to bear on it through our understanding. The Western tradition, as any other, involves a certain interpretation of the world that is embodied in certain forms of expression. We can, and no doubt should, argue in the abstract about whether the Western tradition is superior to others or not, and we should certainly be aware and make students aware that there are rival traditions. We should also seek to arrive at some understanding of them. But it is absurd not to concentrate on understanding our tradition, since it is the tradition that structures our world. To be intelligent in our world is to understand that tradition.

Farewell to Four Siblings

At the outset of this argument I introduced four siblings and raised the question of which, if any, of those individuals we should be inclined to call intelligent. My guess is that as a matter of fact most people, if they were to meet such people briefly, would be inclined to judge the brother with the happy knack of repartee as the most intelligent; longer acquaintance might incline some to estimate the relatively weighty and worldly-wise business woman as more intelligent. Whether one judged the academic brother to be particularly intelligent would no doubt be governed by one's own knowledge of, and attitude to, academic study.

The other sister might impress, but it is unlikely that many would feel able to make a judgement on her intelligence from a brief meeting alone.

Such speculation is, of course, just that and should be fairly rapidly set aside. I merely wish to hint at the possibility that our judgements as to people's intelligence are likely to be coloured by such factors as their liveliness, their seriousness, and the extent to which their interests and values coincide with our own. It is also worth making the point that our judgements of these same people will be affected by whether we experience them exhibiting their various qualities and characteristics, or merely read descriptions of them. My point was, partly, that if you actually met these people, you might be inclined to judge the gardener to be the most intelligent (presumably because the vivacity, good humour and wit would strike you forcefully), whereas you would not necessarily do so on the basis of the written descriptions (presumably because more information is provided, some of which cannot be readily perceived on brief acquaintance).

As to reactions on reading the descriptions provided, readers must judge for themselves; but I should be surprised if, were we to research the matter systematically, we did not find people fairly equally divided between considering one of the older three as relatively intelligent, while the younger sister would come out a poor fourth. If this were the case, it would, I suggest, be largely due to the fact that a lot of people associate intelligence primarily with quick wit, a lot primarily with proven career ability, particularly in business and management, and a lot with academic success. By contrast, few seem to associate the kind of questioning, dogged determination, and willingness to learn new things, that one may suppose lie behind the younger sister's career pattern, with intelligence. I doubt whether many people would think the various clues about personality that I included had much to do with the matter.

But enough idle speculation. If the argument that I have advanced has any merit, it follows that, whatever people might in fact be inclined to do, the descriptions given are insufficient in every case to allow us to conclude that the individual *is* particularly intelligent, but, in the case of the gardener and the businesswoman, are sufficient to allow us to conclude that they *are not*. This conclusion is at bottom a matter of definition (what some people strangely call a matter of 'mere' definition, even though it takes rather a lot of argument, patience, and time to arrive at a definition). They cannot be regarded as intelligent on the account given in these pages, because we are told, though not in precisely these words, that they lack the kind and breadth of understanding that has been written into the concept of intelligence.

The interesting question at this stage is not whether the claim that they are not particularly intelligent is true. That question, as we have insisted all along, is meaningless on the conceptual level, and we are not here concerned with the empirical question of whether, notwithstanding the descriptions, these people do as a matter of fact display intelligence (in some other unspecified sense). The interesting question is whether, and, if so, why, on further reflection, and in the light of what has been argued in these pages, we should change our mind.

In plain language what has been said about the gardening brother is that he has a particular talent (for horticulture), has knowledge of a particular matter (religion), is a decent man, and is prone to swift and amusing repartee. Now it is surely only the last quality that tempts people to see him as intelligent. (By the other criteria, virtually everybody would be equally intelligent.) And the reason it does so, is that, whether consciously or unconsciously, many people are committed to the generic fallacy: the false idea that mental capacities can exist independently of particular contexts. The witty riposte to our clumsy greeting, the amusing twist to a commonplace remark, are taken to be indicative of a general ability to be quick, incisive, to the point, and so on. I have questioned whether such qualities should necessarily be associated with intelligence, but the more immediate point is that since this common presumption is false, we have no good reason to make the judgement. The wit of this individual is, from what we are told, confined to the ability to respond wittily to everyday, trivial, and simple matters. It is a knack on a par with the ability to do crossword puzzles, play Scrabble, or make puns or anagrams. This person may be very likeable, may be preferable in various ways to a number of more intelligent people, may be any number of good things, and certainly has qualities. But, for all his good qualities, his lack of a specific range of understanding makes him ultimately unreliable - an unknown quantity. This is where the value of intelligence comes in, or, to put it another way, where we see one of the reasons for defining intelligence in one way rather than another: this kindly person, who amuses us all, lacks the understanding that would allow us to predict how he would react to new or changed circumstances or to questions of overriding importance.

Mutatis mutandis, much the same can be said of the elder sister, save that, in place of a ready wit, she parades a degree of knowledge about the world of business and, by extension, politics. But, like the gardener, she is not in any position to increase her or our understanding of major political, social, or personal issues.

The remaining brother and sister have been described in such a way that they could turn out to be relatively intelligent, but we cannot possibly know that from the descriptions alone, because the descriptions are only tangentially and contingently related to the definition of intelligence. The academic brother may be intelligent, because his academic success may have incorporated the development of broad understanding along the way. But it might not have done. Certainly, the definition of intelligence given was not a definition in terms of academic qualifications or academic study. Explicit reference was made to study of literature and history in the case of the sister, but that fails to establish her intelligence, since the claim was neither that such study was necessary to developing intelligence, nor that it was sufficient. It was argued that it seemed reasonable to suppose that it would in general be sensible to initiate children into such study, if we wished to take active steps to promote their intelligence. In this case, the study may have contributed to the development of intelligence, but we cannot know that without coming to know the sister.

Judging whether individuals are more or less intelligent depends first and foremost, not upon a check-list of their characteristics, but upon our elucidating a clear conception of intelligence. In doing that, as well as meeting the formal requirements of clarity, coherence, completeness, and compatibility, our analysis must take account of the ways things are (as far as we can judge). Crucial in that respect, in this instance, is the fact that so-called mental skills such as 'critical thinking' and 'understanding' are not generic. Crucial also is the fact that some traditions of inquiry are both distinctive and powerful in ways that others are not. With this in mind, we can articulate a concept of intelligence, but it is one that makes a brief meeting, a brief description, or a brief intelligence test all equally irrelevant ways of judging intelligence. To judge the intelligence of people, it is necessary to have extensive knowledge of their understanding.

Notes and references

1. The reference point is, in particular, the post-Second World War years, especially the Sixties.
2. This is *not* to say that sorting out a few logical steps would solve the world's problems, as Kieran Egan perversely suggests. Nothing I have written should be taken to deny the significance of such things as weakness of will, emotion, passion, individual experience and circumstance, and so forth, despite the fact that I deliberately emphasize the value of rational intelligence. It *is* to say that a great deal of seeming difference of opinion and actual opposition could be at best removed and at worst alleviated by rather more logical understanding.
3. For further discussion of this topic, see Barrow, R., (1981), *Injustice, Inequality and Ethics*, Brighton, Sussex: Wheatsheaf.
4. Some (such as, you guessed it, K.E.) might prefer me to have given more citations of particular views and arguments for them. But I am not concerned to develop the relevant academic context so much as to deal with the ideas themselves.
5. Fukuyama, F., (1992), *The End of History and the Last Man*, London: Hamish Hamilton.
6. See further, e.g., Cotterill, R., (1989), *No Ghost in the Machine*, London: Heinemann.
7. See in particular the celebrated satire, Benjamin, H., 'The Saber-tooth Curriculum', in Golby, M., Greenwald, J., and West, R. (eds), (1975), *Curriculum Design*, London: Croom Helm.
8. Kieran Egan makes the point that 'the universities of Nazi Germany were full of such people'. In so far as this observation reminds us that intellect alone is not enough, since we can be driven by fear, lust, etc., to do that which we otherwise abominate, the point is well taken. But rather more important is the point that under Hitler - as with Stalin and Mao - it was precisely this voice that was silenced in the universities.

9. Kieran Egan, the value of whose caution, conservatism, and correctness in redressing my lack of all three will by now be apparent to the alert reader of these notes, comments, 'Kuhn argues otherwise'. However nothing in Kuhn, T.S., (1962), *The Structure of Scientific Revolutions*, Chicago: University of Chicago Press, has ever led me to alter my contention that, e.g., current medical knowledge represents an advance on the medicine of Rousseau's day in a 'fairly straightforward way'.